First and Second Samuel

INTERPRETATION

BIBLE STUDIES

First and Second Samuel

DAVID C. HESTER

WJK WESTMINSTER
JOHN KNOX PRESS
LOUISVILLE • KENTUCKY

The photographs on pages 7, 26, 40, 61, 71, 89, and 94 are courtesy of SuperStock, Inc.

Page 26: Samuel at Ramah (James Tissot, 1836–1902; Jewish Museum, New York). Page 40: Abraham's Sacrifice (Rembrandt Harmensz van Rijn, 1606–69; Hermitage Museum, St. Petersburg). Page 61: Ark of the Covenant (James Tissot; Jewish Museum, New York). Page 71: Bathsheba Mourns Her Husband (James Tissot; Jewish Museum, New York). Page 78: Auschwitz (Instytut Pamieci Narodowej/Institute of National Memory, Poland; courtesy of USHMM Photo Archives). Page 94: Absalom (James Tissot; Jewish Museum, New York).

Book design by Drew Stevens
Cover design by Pam Poll
Cover illustration by Robert Stratton

First edition
Published by Westminster John Knox Press
Louisville, Kentucky

This book is printed on acid-free paper that meets the American National Standards Institute Z39.48 standard. ♾

PRINTED IN THE UNITED STATES OF AMERICA

05 06 07 08 09 — 10 9 8 7 6 5 4 3 2

Library of Congress Cataloging-in-Publication Data

A catalog record for this book is available from the Library of Congress.

ISBN 0-664-23024-5

Contents

Series Introduction

The Bible has long been revered for its witness to God's presence and redeeming activity in the world; its message of creation and judgment, love and forgiveness, grace and hope; its memorable characters and stories; its challenges to human life; and its power to shape faith. For generations people have found in the Bible inspiration and instruction, and, for nearly as long, commentators and scholars have assisted students of the Bible. This series, Interpretation Bible Studies (IBS), continues that great heritage of scholarship with a fresh approach to biblical study.

Designed for ease and flexibility of use for either personal or group study, IBS helps readers not only to learn about the history and theology of the Bible, understand the sometimes difficult language of biblical passages, and marvel at the biblical accounts of God's activity in human life, but also to accept the challenge of the Bible's call to discipleship. IBS offers sound guidance for deepening one's knowledge of the Bible and for faithful Christian living in today's world.

IBS was developed out of three primary convictions. First, the Bible is the church's scripture and stands in a unique place of authority in Christian understanding. Second, good scholarship helps readers understand the truths of the Bible and sharpens their perception of God speaking through the Bible. Third, deep knowledge of the Bible bears fruit in one's ethical and spiritual life.

Each IBS volume has ten brief units of key passages from a book of the Bible. By moving through these units, readers capture the sweep of the whole biblical book. Each unit includes study helps, such as maps, photos, definitions of key terms, questions for reflection, and suggestions for resources for further study. In the back of each volume is a Leader's Guide that offers helpful suggestions on how to use IBS.

The Interpretation Bible Studies series grows out of the well-known Interpretation commentaries (John Knox Press), a series that helps preachers and teachers in their preparation. Although each IBS volume bears a deep kinship to its companion Interpretation commentary, IBS can stand alone. The reader need not be familiar with the Interpretation commentary to benefit from IBS. However, those who want to discover even more about the Bible will benefit by consulting Interpretation commentaries too.

Through the kind of encounter with the Bible encouraged by the Interpretation Bible Studies, the church will continue to discover God speaking afresh in the scriptures.

Introduction to
First and Second Samuel

Like the other volumes in the Interpretation Bible Studies series, this one is offered as a companion for your journey—in this case, through two books of the Bible. But, more personally, it grows out of teaching and learning from an adult Sunday school class in a local church. Readers will hear more about this group and their significant contributions along the way. But I mention it now simply to underscore how much, as in any Bible study, what we learn depends on the conversations we have with others. Understanding scripture is a work shared by the community of faith, and this volume is offered most especially to help in that sacred work of grace.

However you make the journey through Samuel, whether in a group or in personal study at home, the end or purpose of it is really not so much a "study of" two books of our Bible, as if to hold them at arm's length and examine them objectively. Rather, these books are scripture for us; they are *ours* and the story we will hear is our story. We are subjects in this story, so it is impossible to hold them at much distance. What we really want at the end of study is understanding: knowledge not only of the books but also of ourselves and, ultimately, knowledge of God knowing us. That means we must involve ourselves in learning how and what these texts in Samuel mean. And that requires a conversational relationship with the texts, one another, our church's traditions, and the reality we know from daily life. This book cannot provide all of that. But it can lead toward your own discovery of such conversation partners for yourself and suggest some meanings for faith and the life of faith appropriate to selected passages from the Samuel narrative.

If you have looked at the Contents, I hope you have noticed that our study begins with a song of thanksgiving and praise (Hannah's Song in 1 Sam. 2:1–10) and ends with a song of praise and thanksgiving (David's Hymn of Praise in 2 Samuel 22). Joy, celebration, and promise mark the beginning and the end of the Samuel stories, counterbalancing a great deal of divine and human discouragement, fear, disappointment, betrayal, and heartache found in between. Israel's faithful witnesses have preserved for us here memories of a time of war and the threat of destruction at the hands of politically and militarily superior neighbors, and of Israel's response to that threat in the creation of central leadership in the person and office of a king. But kingship is a highly ambiguous solution to the problems of the people of God, as we will see. The writer of First and Second Samuel holds the behavior of the participants in Israel's story accountable to God, the Holy One of Israel, from the ordinary Israelite to the king. In particular, the standard by which judgment occurs throughout the narrative is the *Torah,* or "Instruction," of the Mosaic covenant. Kingship, in the writer's view, is a dangerous invitation to compromise the commandments and statutes that constitute *Torah,* most especially the commandment against idolatry. As with other Bible narratives, then, those in Samuel are about humankind, God, and politics, and the complex ways these strands weave together into the web of life in which first Israel and now we practice our faith.

First and Second Samuel in fact are part of an even greater collection of testimonies called "the Deuteronomic History." You will read much about this writer's work and viewpoint in chapters that follow. Here I mention it only to set the context for the Samuel books. This ancient historian writes, unlike modern historians, with identity questions foremost in mind, rather than offering well-documented and researched description and objective analysis of Israel's past. Deuteronomic history begins with

> For further reading on First and Second Samuel, see Walter Brueggemann, *First and Second Samuel,* Interpretation (Louisville, Ky.: John Knox Press, 1990); Eugene H. Peterson, *First and Second Samuel,* Westminster Bible Companion (Louisville, Ky.: Westminster John Knox Press, 1999); and David Payne, *I & II Samuel,* Daily Study Bible (Philadelphia: Westminster Press, 1982).

Joshua and Judges and extends beyond First and Second Samuel through First and Second Kings. This is a history written to make a theological point to Israel in exile, and that purpose shapes the narratives in First and Second Samuel and must therefore also shape our reading of them.

If love, violence, social crisis, and political intrigue constitute a perfect formula for Hollywood or television success in attracting and holding an audience, a reading of First and Second Samuel should prove no less exciting and engaging. The situations and human pathos visible in this narrative are fully contemporary, despite their ancient dress and color. As with other scripture, there is no need to *make the Bible relevant* here. Rather, our need is to listen carefully and see clearly the relevance of the narrative that reaches out for us in our modern life and world. How can we see through the Samuel narrative what God wants from us as disciples of Christ, how God calls us to be and act in this chapter of the ongoing story of the redeeming and reconciling of God's world? How can we hear in these stories Israel's witness to God's relationship with God's people in order that this testimony may become truthful for us?

Because Samuel is scripture for us, as testimony Samuel is normative for us as Christians. That is, it tells us what the community of faith believes is true about God and how God relates to those in covenant with God, with others, and with creation more generally; and it tells us what kind of response is normative behavior for those in relationship with God. In offering this testimony, how-

> **Deuteronomic History**
> I.   The Age of Moses—Deuteronomy
> II. The Age of Joshua—Joshua
> III. The Age of the Judges—Judges, 1 Samuel
> IV. The Age of the Kings—2 Samuel, 1 and 2 Kings

ever, it does not say exactly what God may or may not do; it does not tell us all there is to tell about God. Testimony does not limit the freedom of God. Nor does testimony prescribe exactly what those who believe it to be true should do in particular circumstances. Testimony is normative; it is not prescriptive. It provides us with truthful images and accounts, and invites us to examine contemporary situations in their light, looking at them not as historical duplicates but as historical analogies, similar but different, alike yet unlike. Each unit presented here invites dialogue between human experience, biblical interpretation, and suggested ways the text may provide light on contemporary life issues that are analogous to those in the text.

In the end, the theological theme that marks our way through First and Second Samuel concerns the persistent drive from Hannah's Song in 1 Samuel 2 to David's Song in 2 Samuel 22 to balance the gift of life from God and the promise of God's steadfast love with the ever-present temptation to take control, to usurp God's authority.

3

The practical demands of changing times as Israel grew from tribal peoples to a nation among nations always invited taking matters into human hands. Nor did the covenant relationship with God suggest that the people of God had no responsibility for governing their lives together and with their neighbors. But where, the narratives ask us, is the line between acting within covenant relationship and usurping the intentions of God? The drive to kingship in David and the attendant joy and heartache serve as a means for the Deuteronomic writer to work out this very human and divine dilemma. What is our role; what belongs to God? That's the question for First and Second Samuel, and for us as well.

I conclude with a note to aid readers of the volume. Throughout, to honor the tradition of Israel and Judaism that the pronunciation of the sacred name of God be avoided, I have left the four letters of the name without vowels, YHWH. This is the Hebrew expression that in English translations is often rendered by Lord in all capital letters, LORD. Secondly, in order to underscore the unity of the scriptures, rather than referring to them in the traditional fashion as the "old" and "new" testaments, I have referred to them as the First and Second Testaments. This is a practice shared by many in biblical studies today, and is particularly appropriate, I believe, within a Reformed theology that has historically denied that the First Testament is superseded as God's Word by the Second. Finally, where dates appear that are before the first century, I have dated them B.C.E.—"Before the Common Era," indicating time that is marked and shared by Christianity and Judaism. Christians belong to the people of God, together with Jewish brothers and sisters. The common dating underscores faithfully our relationship in time, rather than marking the time by difference as A.D. and B.C. do. I have put these notes last because I hope to indicate the place these particular writing decisions ought to play in deciding on the usefulness and value of this study guide. I do not mean them as "stumbling blocks." But neither can I deny their significance to me as I have written.

My hope is that you will enjoy working through these chapters as

Want to Know More?

About leading Bible study groups? See Roberta Hestenes, *Using the Bible in Groups* (Philadelphia: Westminster Press, 1983).

About Deuteronomic History? See Werner H. Schmidt, *Old Testament Introduction,* 2d ed. (Louisville, Ky.: Westminster John Knox Press, 1999), 136–59.

much as the Sunday school class and I did in engaging in the Bible study that preceded this writing. May God bless you in your study and search for meaning important to you in the scripture that is First and Second Samuel.

1 Samuel 2:1–10

Hannah's Song

Our Bible study begins and will end with a song of praise celebrating the graceful work of God in the life of Israel. Both songs belong in worship, so figuratively all the crises, challenges, betrayals, disappointments, and surprises that fall between the first and last chapters of Samuel are set in worship, too. That's how it is for us as well: a song of praise for the beginning of life, at birth but also on every day thereafter; and a song of thanksgiving and praise at the end of life, not as a king like David but as a child of God, like David.

To comprehend the celebration of 1 Samuel 2:1–10 requires at least a quick scan of chapter 1 for the story line that brings us here. What calls forth this hymn of praise is not self-evident from the hymn's contents, which are a clue to its history of development. We will return to that matter a bit later. For the sake of hearing and responding to the story before us in Samuel, the events of chapter 1 and the direction the story will take in future chapters is more important.

Chapter 1 introduces us to the family of the child to be born: his father, Elkanah; his mother, Hannah; his father's other wife, Peninnah, and her anonymous children. These are the human players in the drama to unfold; and, though highly important now, they will not remain on stage long. The writer tells us just enough: We know who they are but we are not allowed to stay fixed on them. Our attention will be drawn elsewhere. Elkanah is portrayed as a loving husband and, importantly, a righteous man before God, keeping all God's commandments carefully. His is a patriarchal family in a patriarchal society, where having multiple wives is ordinary and where male children count for more than female children. That may cause us to bristle as we read it from our point of view, but it is part of the reality of the ancient world to which Israel belongs.

Peninnah is a character to dislike. As the wife who has borne heirs for Elkanah, she gloats over the barren Hannah and ridicules her at every opportunity. She is like the favored child who taunts and teases and makes the misery of another all the more deeply felt. She is on and off stage quickly in this drama, thankfully.

Hannah, on the other hand, is a hero- ine of faith. Her circumstance, in the beginning, seems hopeless. She is barren and, as noted twice by the text, her barrenness is attributable, from her per- spective, to God, who has "shut her womb" (1:5, 6). Later she describes her situation as being "forgotten" and "for- saken" by YHWH, and in her desperate prayer (1:11) she begs God to remember her and grant her what she so urgently wants: a male child. Her barrenness is really evidence of what is mak- ing her heartsick and depressed: being out of God's favor, unable to

> "Hannah, for her part, while she may have loved her husband, still needed chil- dren, and not only for her personal emo- tional fulfillment. In her society a woman's prestige was based at least partly on her demonstrated ability to produce off- spring."—Jo Ann Hackett, in *Women's Bible Commentary*, expanded edition, 95.

bring forth life that God has "knit together" in her womb. Despite all apparent hopelessness, Hannah hopes and prays and turns *to*, not away *from*, the Holy One who has closed her womb, for she is not willing to grant that power to anyone or anything else.

God does not disappoint her. In "due time" she bears the child she hoped and prayed for. As a sign of her joy and grat- itude, she dedicates the boy, Samuel, to God and leaves him as a gift before the altar in care of the priest, Eli, to raise him to serve YHWH. Now the drama reaches its true beginning, and Hannah announces it with a hymn of praise. The hopelessness with which the story opened in chapter one, manifest in Hannah's refusal to eat and her deep,

long-suffered depression (1:7, 11), is transformed into celebration and joy and a faithfulness that allows her to empty herself of the long-awaited gift-child, returning him to the Giver. This transformation, Hannah acknowledges, does not come through her strength or that of any other; it happens only by grace, by the sheer will of God (2:9). The faithful woman, whose name "Hannah" means "grace" in Hebrew, having begun in barrenness now lives in fullness—all, our story affirms, by the work and will of our grace-full God.

Before we look more closely at 2:1–10, however, we need to address the boiling question that pours over this characterization of Hannah. If we do not tackle it now, then what we see in the story as meaningful and true for us, commanding for us, may be skewed by our frustration with the depiction by the narrator and writer of barren Hannah, Elkanah's wife.

> **The Stigma of Barrenness**
>
> "In the absence of knowledge about the biological process of conception and the reasons for infertility, ancient cultures usually held the women responsible for a couple's inability to conceive children. Her 'failure' was often interpreted as God's judgment against her, by which she brought suffering and shame on her husband."—Sharon H. Ringe, *Luke*, Westminster Bible Companion (Louisville, Ky.: Westminster John Knox Press, 1995), 28.

Two things rub us as wrong in this matter-of-fact description of Elkanah's family: first, that Hannah's inability to have a child—and, more specifically, a male child—so dramatically marginalizes her in her society. As a childless wife, she is a second-class citizen and the object of family ridicule and—though the story does not say so, we might expect—public pity and gossip. We want to protest, "It's not her fault!" Moreover, we wonder how a society, especially one formed in faith and guided by divine instruction, could be so insensitive and cruel. That it is so blatantly patriarchal goes a long way toward explaining the social role of women as child-bearers. The logic that follows is relatively simple but mistaken: If women are child-bearers, and if a woman does not bear a child, then she is less than a woman. In the hierarchical arrangement of society, if Hannah is not a woman and wife, then what is she?

Many women and their partners in our congregations today struggle with the grief and longing that accompanies wanting to have a child and not being able to bear one. To them this treatment of Hannah must seem very personal and real, having felt the "What's wrong with you?" questions, even if unspoken, from friends and especially from parents hopeful for grandchildren. For many, the coming of children still completes their marriage and family, which without children would remain unfinished. To be sure, more means are available to us today for understanding and for providing solutions to infertility. But that should not obscure the rightful protest we may raise concerning Hannah's marginalization in her own home and community and the continuing marginalization of women who cannot or do not wish to bear children in our own communities. That Hannah's situation is positively resolved does not mitigate the suffering endured over the years.

The second matter in Hannah's story that bothers us is this: The narrator, her antagonist Peninnah, and Hannah herself all attribute the cause of her barrenness to YHWH, who "closed her womb" (1:5). Hannah's deep faith allows for none beside YHWH (2:2). The resounding theme of Hannah's song is the transformative power of the God of Israel, who "weighs actions . . . breaks the bows of the mighty . . . kills and brings to life . . . and . . . makes poor and makes rich" (see 2:2–8). God is responsible for everything, and nothing happens by chance or bad luck—that's key in Hannah's theology. Therefore, barrenness means "God has shut her womb." Yet she becomes a voice of God's praise, extolling God's power and generosity in her song when her barrenness is ended. We want to know why: Why was she *made* barren by a loving, grace-full Deliverer? How could this Holy One, who shows so much favor to the lowly and needy, as her praise hymn joyfully proclaims, be responsible for Hannah's emptiness and pain? If the Righteous One takes care of the faithful, how could faithful Hannah be left in depression and ridicule? Those are some of our questions, if the Sunday school class I teach is any measure. If "barrenness" has other explanations for us today, the power of God to dramatically change the circumstances in which we live remains a valuable and important part of Christian belief. We know of personal circumstances that do not end as happily as Hannah's, where hymns of praise remain forever hard to sing, or where they must be sung without life's painful circumstances being turned around and upside down, as Hannah's song describes. So when we think about it as a symbol or metaphor for a host of experiences of pain and deprivation, deep pangs of emptiness, dark, impenetrable depression, and social ostracization, Hannah's barrenness raises questions about justice in our lives and world and, in particular, the justice of God. Whatever our experiences of unreasonable suffering, whatever our feelings about God's accountability for "dark nights of the soul," tragic circumstances of life, and "natural disaster"—we bring all of that when we read Hannah's story and listen to her "new song" of deliverance from the darkness.

It is always dangerous to judge the behavior of another society in another age, particularly when the accounts we have—for example, the story before us—are limited, and make little or no effort to explain themselves. Nevertheless, when we read accounts of social structure or personal behavior that we find highly questionable or objectionable from our point of view, these accounts can help us see similar circumstances in our own setting and motivate us to correction and reformation. Similarly, if we do not agree with the ancient story's portrayal of God's involvement in the misery of God's people, rather than trying to correct or dismiss that account, it can probe our own views, values, and beliefs. We might ask ourselves: If God is not responsible for our "barrenness," then how do we account for it and what does our accounting say about our view of God's sovereignty and power within human lives and life on earth, more generally?

If we look now carefully at Hannah's Song in 1 Samuel 2:1–10, we have more to learn as we move toward identifying meanings in this story for our lives. To begin with, the setting of the Song, which I have described, would lead us to expect far more in the psalm about barrenness and fruitfulness than we find. One line in verse 5 speaks of barrenness being overcome; that's it. Otherwise the images are generalized, pointing to the dramatic reversal of "the way things have been" in society (vv. 2–8). In the context, only one verse (v. 1) is apparently in Hannah's voice: "My heart exults in YHWH (NRSV, "the LORD") . . . because I rejoice in your salvation" (reading with the Revised Standard Version and the Hebrew text). As expected in a psalm of praise, it is what YHWH has done that is praiseworthy, it is who God is that is remarkable. So it is Hannah's Song not because it is *about* Hannah or her particular circumstance, but because she praises God through the community of faith's language of praise, rejoicing that she belongs to such a God. She is motivated to praise, to be sure, by the end of her barrenness *and* by her successful keeping of her vow to dedicate the unborn child to the service of God all the days of his life. The story of what has happened to Hannah now joins the community of faith's witness to the transformative power of God, the unaccountable grace of God, and the legendary faith of the mother of Samuel.

> "Hannah sings a very special song with reference to a concrete miracle. In doing so, however, she joins her voice to a song Israel has already long been singing. Israel is peculiarly a community of doxology. Its life consists in praise to God for what God has done and for what God characteristically continues to do. Thus Hannah sings no new song; she appropriates a song already known in Israel."—Brueggemann, *First and Second Samuel*, Interpretation, 16.

Most striking to a reader is verse 10, which suddenly shoves our attention far ahead of the story, with the pious affirmation, "[YHWH] will give strength to his king, and exalt the power of his anointed." Most biblical scholars point to this phrase in particular as evidence that the Song of Hannah is a public psalm of praise that has been placed here in the Samuel story by the Deuteronomic writer of the narrative. This historian writes from the vantage point of the end of kingship in Israel, several hundred years after Samuel's birth, with Israel in exile in Babylon—a time marked by death and hopelessness. That leaves the question of how old the psalm is, or what its original setting was, unanswered, and that need not bother us. We are concerned with the place and function of Hannah's Song in the context of the first three chapters of Samuel and beyond.

Hannah celebrates God's deliverance and, in particular, God's power to transform and reverse present circumstances of oppression to bring joy and fullness to those who suffer deprivation, loss, and hopelessness. The song is timely, since Israel—as described by the Deuteronomic Historian whose story starts with Joshua—finds itself in Hannah's day with little or no hope for a future. The last half of the book of Judges portrays just how lawless and self-destructive the period was. Now Israel waits for a king, one last hope for stable leadership that will enable the fledgling nation to withstand the power of the Philistines and live as an equal among the surrounding nations. In Walter Brueggemann's felicitous phrase, it is a time of "troubled waiting" (Brueggemann, 11). Hannah's "barrenness" and accompanying sense of hopelessness and despair serve as a metaphor for the crisis in which all of Israel finds itself, as it waits for one more deed of deliverance and gift of grace (*hanah*) from our steadfastly loving God.

Hannah's Song sings, then, of the hoped-for reversal of the present painful, oppressive, fearful times. It sings of a future time when the reign of God becomes the rule of life on earth. It sings of a coming Messiah, YHWH's anointed, who as God's instrument of justice and love will lead Israel in the transformation of "things as they are" into things as God intends them to be. In the near sight, the king anticipated in

> "What we have here is not a charming, idyllic narrative with a happy ending and piety rewarded. The psalm puts the birth, and hence the life, of Samuel in the context of the all-powerful saving acts of God. These stories are intended to be history, the history of God's dealings with the chosen people."—Hertzberg, *I and II Samuel: A Commentary*, 31.

Hannah's hymn is David, who is at the heart and soul of the Samuel narrative. The hymn also celebrates Samuel the king-maker,

Hannah's gift from God and gift to Israel at this critical moment in Israel's history.

As we read, we cannot help but think of Jesus Messiah or, in Greek, Christ. Israel's hope for a righteous Messiah to establish the reign of God on earth was not exhausted by David, though David remained an idealized Messiah figure throughout Israel's history. Jesus of Nazareth, our Messiah, is connected by the Gospel writers to David's line through the genealogies of Jesus in Matthew 1 and Luke 3:23–38, as well as the birth story in Luke 1:26–38. It is their testimony that Jesus is the long-awaited Messiah, born to set people free and to establish God's rule of justice and love on earth. Indeed, Jesus too comes at a time in Israel's life when oppression, poverty, pain, and fear characterize the national life and the personal lives of the majority of the children of Abraham and Sarah. Jesus knows, as Hannah did, the experience of the *absence of God,* as well as the presence of God. Through these "valleys of deep darkness" (Psalm 23) Jesus keeps faith, as Hannah does, believing that God can and may still turn things around, steadfast love responding to steadfast hope. There are, of course, many other places where the testimony of the Christian community connects Jesus Messiah to the household of David. You might want to use a concordance, which you may find in your church library or perhaps borrow from your pastor, to identify these passages and see how the early church celebrated Jesus' relationship with the house of David.

As you read Hannah's Song it may have seemed a familiar hymn. No wonder. The content of Hannah's poem is strongly paralleled in Mary's acclamation upon receiving the news from the angel Gabriel that she was to bear the long-awaited Messiah. We call her song of joy and celebration "The Magnificat" after the first line of the poem: "My soul *magnifies* the Lord, and my spirit rejoices in God my Savior" (Luke 1:46b–47). Compare with Hannah's words in 1 Samuel 2:1: "My heart exults in YHWH; my strength is exalted in my God . . . because I rejoice in your victory (or salvation)" (author's translation). Most biblical scholars agree that the author of the song in Luke likely consciously borrowed from the psalm of praise in 1 Samuel 2. That does not diminish the creativity or truthfulness of the Lukan author one bit. On the contrary, by adapting Hannah's Song to Mary's situation, we who celebrate the birth of Jesus Messiah and God's saving work wrought through him are joined to the earlier testimony to God's faithfulness. We join centuries of hope born of belief that God will make right what is wrong in our world, and overturn all that destroys and causes grief in the human community. Though for different reasons, according to the narratives, Mary and Hannah are both childless and both are people of deep, life-giving faith. That hope for salvation could come to life through either of them seems impossible. Apart from God's role in the human narrative—ancient or modern—transformation from death to life, from emptiness to fullness, is impossible. But, praise God, Mary and Hannah are indeed bearers of children of promise and hope. For nothing is impossible with God.

> "This story began with Hannah weeping. It ends with Hannah singing. Hannah's sung prayer is a powerful witness to a life lived in intense interaction with God."—Peterson, *First and Second Samuel*, Westminster Bible Companion, 24.

Now, what about us? Throughout this study I have hinted at several very real and very modern human concerns that the narrative of Samuel, as a whole, and that of Hannah, in particular, raise for faithful reflection. I indicated that Hannah's Song must be understood in its context. In its immediate context it is a mediating chapter between the surprising story of barren Hannah—whose persistent faith participated in God overcoming her childlessness with the gift of Samuel—and the account in chapter 3 of Samuel's development into a faithful and righteous prophet of God. Borrowing from Brueggemann, I called attention to the "troubling times" in which Hannah and her family lived and to the sense of "waiting" for a Messiah that gave people hope and cause to think their present unbearable circumstances might soon be overcome: a time of "troubled waiting." That hope is visible in Hannah's Song in the last verse. She, in fact, is the mother of Samuel, who will anoint in his lifetime two kings, the second of whom, David, is the central figure in the Samuel narrative. Hannah's Song is truly an affirmation of faith and a declaration of hope. The Holy One of Israel, who has brought life to Hannah, will do the same for those who are barren of hope for a future free of the oppressive, marginalizing, fearful conditions of their present lives. That's gospel—"good news" for Israel under threat of dissolution at the time the Samuel story opens, and it is good news for the exiles perhaps 500 hundred years later, for whom the Deuteronomic Historian fashioned the whole narrative through First and Second Kings.

I suggest Hannah's story and her Song remain "gospel" for people of faith in our day. To begin with, Hannah is a model of persistent faith. Brueggemann and others are correct to affirm that the story here—as everywhere in the Bible—is first and foremost a story about God's hearing the cry of distressed and bereaved and enslaved people, and turning the world upside down to find justice and love. Yet it is also a story about Hannah's faith, her relentless effort to overcome her unbearable situation. We can relate to her circumstances and her feelings easily, though our situation may be far different from the cause of suffering she protests. If the story of *Samuel* resounds with the presence of God, human beings in it, like Hannah, know equally well the absence of God. What makes her a strong witness to faith is her ability, in the depths of despair, to pray and verbally pound on Heaven's door to find help from the only One who can ultimately free her from her anguish. She does not pray timidly but boldly and, keep in mind, she begs to be remembered by the very Creator who she also confesses has "closed her womb." This kind of praying and pressing God takes courage—courage born of a faith that knows YHWH has been at the side of Israel in countless situations of oppression and loss.

Want to Know More?

About the use of the letters YHWH? For an accessible explanation, see the annotations on Exodus 3:13–15 in Gail R. O'Day and David L. Petersen, editors, *The Access Bible* (New York: Oxford University Press, 1999), 73–74; James D. Newsome, *Exodus*, Interpretation Bible Studies (Louisville, Ky.: Geneva Press, 1998), 15–25; Terence G. Fretheim, *Exodus*, Interpretation (Louisville, Ky.: John Knox Press, 1991), 62–67. For a thorough discussion, see Rainer Albertz, *A History of Israelite Religion in the Old Testament Period*, vol. 1, Old Testament Library (Louisville, Ky.: Westminster John Knox Press, 1994), 49–51.

About the role of women in the Old Testament? See Carol A. Newsom and Sharon H. Ringe, eds., *Women's Bible Commentary*, expanded edition (Louisville, Ky.: Westminster John Knox Press, 1998), 251–59; for an excellent overview, see Evelyn and Frank Stagg, *Woman in the World of Jesus* (Philadelphia: Westminster Press, 1978).

Hannah's faithfulness encourages us to take a close look at the role our faith plays in our lives, particularly in those terrible situations that occur to all of us that challenge our beliefs. In the Hannah narrative, there is a straight line in the writer's view between what God did *to* her and what God did *for* her. Her suffering, in retrospect, leads to something wonderful: She is the mother of a child who will always stand in God's favor and be God's voice to Israel. Could she see that during those dark days of not eating, of being distressed, of raging against the ridicule of her rivals? No doubt she could not, anymore than we can see clearly through the tears of our distress. Nevertheless, her commitment to God—even when God was apparently absent—formed a handhold for her, a structure for support and getting through another day. Did her faith finally persuade a begrudging deity to accede to her crying for a child? That, I think, would be a wrong reading of the narrative. Samuel comes to Hannah in God's time, and Hannah is not privy to just when the "right time" may be. But she has in hand and heart her community of faith's testimony about the steadfast, loving, saving God who heard their cries and led them out of Egypt and brought them into this promised land. Our community in Christ has a story, too, which knows of a generous, gracious, and purposeful God, who became incarnate in Jesus Messiah. The challenge to faith is keeping this saving story in heart, mind, and soul in the pits of despair and days of feeling useless or without real purpose in life. In such moments, one part of the story to keep in mind is gracefully given us in this story of Hannah and her Song. Remember Hannah and her bold celebration of the impossible transformed into possibility by our loving and saving God.

 ## Questions for Reflection

1. Do you think that women in today's society who either choose not to or cannot have children are marginalized? Can you think of an instance where a woman you know of was treated as a second-class citizen because she did not have children?
2. Do you accept the statement in 1 Samuel 1:5–6 that God "shut her womb"? If so, why do you think God chose to do that to Hannah? If not, why do you have trouble accepting that statement?
3. Read this passage and then read Luke 1:46–55. In what ways are these songs of praise similar? In what ways are they different?
4. How can Hannah be a model for God's people today?

2

1 Samuel 8:4–22

"Give Us a King"

With the opening words of chapter 8 we have taken a giant step from Samuel's birth story to his old age. In between (particularly chapters 4–6) tribal Israel has moved through perilous times. These have been the days of Eli and his sons ruling as judges over Israel, while Samuel grew to maturity. The enemy dogging the people of God throughout this period is the Philistines, a powerful coastal kingdom unwilling to let Israel settle quietly in the land. On Eli's watch, the Ark of the Covenant—Israel's most sacred symbol of the presence of God—was lost in battle to the Philistines, with the result that nascent Israel was both defeated and humiliated.

Only with the emergence of Samuel as judge (7:3–4) and a ceremony of repentance at Mizpah (7:5–6) was the covenant relationship restored. Subsequently, God responded to Samuel's "crying out" for Israel in the face of another Philistine threat. This time Israel under Samuel prevailed. The narrator tells us that the Philistines were subdued and the people of God lived in peace, with Samuel administering justice throughout the tribes all during his life. That brings us to chapter 8.

Since verses 1–3 are summed up in the words of the elders of Israel in verse 4, we can begin with the latter verse. What they have to say must have been hard for Samuel to hear: "You are old; your children don't walk in your ways, but take bribes and pervert justice; so give us a king to govern us, like the other nations" (v. 5, para-

> "When the people demanded a king, what they had in mind was the impressive display of grandeur that would show that they were as important as the neighboring nations and give them a strong central authority. . . . They wanted a government that had style and clout."—Peterson, *First and Second Samuel*, Westminster Bible Companion, 56.

phrase). The terseness of the elders' demand reflects the anxiety that is growing with Samuel's age. Implicit is the question, "What are we to do for a leader we can trust to do what is right after you, Samuel, are no longer here?" It is a profoundly important question, probably as hard to ask as to hear.

The elders propose a solution that anticipates a future in which Israel will have to take its place within the circle of nations that occupied the ancient Near East and included their nemesis the Philistines. Barely hidden in their proposal is the conclusion that the old way of a loosely bound tribal federation with a charismatic judge at the head will not be adequate in the future. Instead, monarchy and a centralized, unified form of government is demanded by the times and the new situation in tribal Israel. Israel is becoming a nation. It must have national governance able to relate to the other nations; it must have a king to secure national affairs, like the other nations.

Their demand made, the elders of the community now fall silent in the narrative, reappearing only to reiterate the demand for a king in verses 19–20. We, the readers, are invited now to listen to Samuel's dialogue with YHWH regarding what to do with the elders' desire for a monarchy. We are standing with Samuel, YHWH, and the elders at a major turning point in Israel's history. We are watching the end of one institution, judgeship, and the struggle to begin a new institution, monarchy. It is a pivotal moment, with decisions with far-reaching consequences to be made. Samuel does not like the proposal and seeks support in his distaste for the elders' demand from YHWH (v. 6).

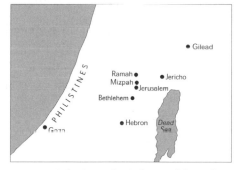

Palestine under Joshua and the Judges

Unfortunately, the narrator skimps on what we are allowed to overhear. We do not know all that Samuel said to YHWH as he reported the matter. But we can guess from YHWH's response that it was not altogether altruistic. Today we might say that Samuel seemed to have "personalized" the demand for a king as a rejection of him as judge, *rather than as a transition from judgeship to kingship.* YHWH sets Samuel straight: "They have not rejected you, but they have rejected me from being king over them" (v. 7). Nor do we know what "all the words of YHWH" included, which Samuel reported to the elders asking him for a king (v. 10). It is hard to imagine that the report to the people began so tersely. It begins without notice of the warning that was coming and without any mention of YHWH's linking the demand for a king with the pattern of rejection and idolatry that plagued the relationship between God and the people from the beginning (v. 8). Nor does Samuel report the most amazing word of YHWH; namely, that Samuel is to listen to their demand and give them a king, as they requested.

> "The worst feature of the elders' demand, in the biblical writer's eyes, was their desire to *be like all the nations* (v. 20). . . . [T]o his own people [God] has given special gifts and higher standards, and it is tragic when they spurn these for no better reason than to be like other people."—David F. Payne, *I & II Samuel*, Daily Study Bible, 43.

Both Samuel and YHWH are struggling in our narrative to make peace with the people's demand for a king and with everything monarchy includes and implies. Amazingly, YHWH grants the request immediately, despite the pain and continuing pattern of unfaithful behavior that it brings. But Samuel cannot seem to bring himself to do as God directs him and "give them a king." Ultimately, he gives the people a one-sided warning against the potential abuse of royal authority. We know, however, from 1 Samuel 10:25, as well as other passages in the First Testament, that the "ways of kingship" included duties as well as rights. At the end of the narrative, Samuel sends the people home without doing as God ordered and appointing for them a king. YHWH will have to take the initiative in king-making; Samuel cannot bring himself to do it. The longest portion of our chapter, verses 11–18, reflects Samuel's effort to dissuade Israel from kingship despite YHWH's word spoken to him three times, commanding him to listen to the people's demand and give them a king.

Samuel, like so many of us, finds it very difficult—maybe even impossible—to let go of long-established patterns of being and doing. Our identity, our self-understanding, and our understanding of the way the world works are all up for grabs, it seems, if we let go of familiar patterns of living. Samuel is not prepared to see judgeship, his lifelong vocation, come to an end, even though YHWH is. God moves ahead of Samuel—ahead of each and all of us—again.

In the long run of the Deuteronomic History, which encompasses *Deuteronomy, Joshua, Judges, 1 and 2 Samuel, and 1 and 2 Kings,* the moment in the story at which we are looking provides an answer to the community of faith's questions about how the monarchy began in Israel. The answer provided is that it began grudgingly, a divine concession to a fearful people of God who thought that becoming *like* other nations would provide them security *among* them. Since monarchies are hereditary in a way judgeships were not, it matters who becomes the first legitimate king. God takes the initiative, through Samuel, of identifying the right person for the role—Saul. But the Deuteronomic Historian knows, as the whole community knows, that David, not Saul, is to be the king whom God favors. Monarchy begins grudgingly, and haltingly, in Israel.

God works God's purpose out, after all, through human beings: people like us, who resist, demand, forget, promise, betray, and like to take control. God, as the narrative makes clear, is profoundly affected by our behavior. God is alternately moved, touched, disturbed, and pleased with what the children of God do and say. We are glimpsing in this scene involving Samuel, the elders, and YHWH, the heart and soul of a God whose steadfast love stoops and bends to nurture a relationship with the people of God. So the monarchy begins, the narrative testifies, grudgingly, haltingly, but ultimately born of the patient love of God, who confides a sense of betrayal to Samuel but overcomes it, once more, with grace.

Nor is God's permission granted without stipulation. The people of God must hear and understand the rights and duties ("the ways of the king") of the kingship here authorized—the potential for evil and for good in centralized and hereditary authority. *Whether a king lives and governs by covenant Torah or abuses power and authority, as Samuel warns in our chapter, becomes the wool by which the Deuteronomic Historian weaves the narrative from here on*. The behavior of the king will determine the fate of the people he rules; his sin weighs against the whole community, while his faithfulness washes over them with divine favor. Remember Samuel's dire warning that closes his speech to the people: "And in that day you will cry out because of your king . . . but the LORD will not answer you" (v. 18). Grace and love do not nullify accountability. We know that, too.

One of the members of our adult Sunday school class studying *Samuel* said when we were talking about this chapter, "This is confusing. If God didn't want a king and if this was such a bad thing to do, why did God 'give in' and why is David such a hero in the Bible?" It is a good

> "It is a torturing dilemma, but the urgencies of human life are strong. And so Samuel is instructed by God to honor the request, but not before painting a grim picture of things to come (vs. 10–18)."—James D. Newsome Jr., *1 & 2 Samuel*, Knox Preaching Guides, John H. Hayes, ed. (Atlanta: John Knox Press, 1982), 35.

question. There are virtually side-by-side in the First Testament passages that warn against the evils of kingship, with its attendant "becoming like all the nations," and other passages that affirm God's authorization of the transition from a tribal society to a monarchy. Our passage has both those elements in it, and some biblical scholars have argued that we are actually seeing here the hands of two "schools of thought" in Israel: one strongly anti-monarchy and the other pro-monarchy. However, that controversy need not concern us here, largely because neither argument can be compellingly supported and neither is necessary to account for the struggle with social transformation to which we are witnesses in chapter 8. The elders' demand, YHWH's plaintive permission, and Samuel's resistance are fully understandable if we take this scene for the intimate exposé that it is.

It may pay, however, for us to pause briefly to look at Deuteronomy 17:14–20, where the limits and responsibilities of kingship are taken up in some detail and where we find, also, the warning edge to them that we find in Samuel's speech in our chapter. Of course there are at least two ways to explain the relation of this passage to 1 Samuel 8:4–22. It could be, and has been, argued that the instruction (in Hebrew, *Torah*) in Deuteronomy 17:14–20 has been written in such a way as to reflect the realities of Israel's history. Israel had kings, no doubt; the Deuteronomic Historian, in this view, is simply "updating" the earlier passage, accommodating what happened and authorizing it as YHWH's *torah*. That would mean that the Deuteronomic passage actually reached its final form *after* Samuel. This argument makes good sense, because we know that the Deuteronomic Historian, like other ancient history writers, used older materials in his narratives.

On the other hand, one might argue that 1 Samuel 8 provides a "case study" of the instruction in Deuteronomy. What is anticipated in Deuteronomy 17:14 is realized in 1 Samuel 8:4; and YHWH, in fact, does take the initiative to choose the one who is to rule over Israel, as the stories of Saul and David will show. This option does not resolve the question of which passage is earlier, historically, nor what part of Deuteronomy 17:14–20 is "original," though it suggests strongly that the Deuteronomic provisions for kingship *in the narrative* preceded the portion of 1 Samuel that we are exploring. In this view, the Deuteronomic Historian has given us a well-linked narrative, with Deuteronomy 17 anticipating 1 Samuel 8, and both of them pointing beyond themselves to the history of the trials of the Israelite community so profoundly shaped by the new structures being put in place in Samuel's old age.

The question of the "historicity" of 1 Samuel 8 is not at issue here. In both of the possible relationships I have sketched between 1 Samuel 8 and Deuteronomy 17, the comparison being made is a *literary* comparison dealing with the texts *as written texts*. The importance for our examining these relationships rests in helping us understand the ambiguous feelings of the Deuteronomic Historian toward monarchy in Israel. The comparison suggests that the Deuteronomic writer was, at best, ill at ease with the possibility that a king or courtiers or the people as a whole could finally resist the temptations to misuse and abuse power and authority entrusted to them by YHWH within their covenant relationship.

The justification offered by the elders in 1 Samuel 8:4 for their demand that Samuel appoint a king rests on the perversity of Samuel's own children, the unreliability of tribal leadership that cannot outlive a generation, and the threat of Philistine power poised to take over the land given Israel. But the counterquestion raised has to do with their trust in and willingness to rely upon the grace and providence of God. Both YHWH and Samuel refer to it, with powerful feelings exposed, naming it "betrayal" and "idolatry." The elders and the people, however, never raise the issue; nor does Samuel as far as we know confront them with it. Nonetheless, at the heart of this narrative is precisely the image of our God, driven to sorrow by the betrayal and habitual idolatry of God's people, yet persistently loving them. Exodus deliverance dared to dream of a future in which those brought out of slavery would never return to it—in any form, including serving foreign gods. Deuteronomy imagined a nonhierarchical future society in which the people of God would be led by a king who was "equal before the *Torah*" (see Deut. 17:14–20) with everyone else. Loyalty of the servant king to YHWH would bind him not to royal privilege but to humble service on behalf of God's own. For this reason, David, as we shall see, is held up as the paradigm of kingship. The moment in 1 Samuel 8:4–22 that holds us rapt left readers before us wondering, "Now, how will things go? What will happen to God's dreams for God's people?" Now it is our question to be worked out in our time, as the story of God's covenant people continues to unfold.

What sort of Word from God may these words of the Deuteronomic narrator offer us? What meanings may be here for a

> "Samuel prayed to the Lord, and the Lord said to Samuel, 'Listen to the voice of the people in all that they say to you; for they have not rejected you, but they have rejected me from being king over them.'"—1 Samuel 8:6b–7

contemporary Christian living in a republic whose people themselves have historically had a love-hate relationship with monarchy? At one end of our national story is a Declaration of Independence from the rule of all foreign monarchs and a Constitution intended to prevent power being concentrated in the hands of any domestic executive. Nevertheless, the "course of human events" in the United States between then and now has produced occasional fondness for seeing the power and authority of the Executive branch increased, only to be followed by an ebb of anxiety away from the White House to another branch. Among our people are hundreds of thousands who have experienced life within monarchies without fear of power abuse and perhaps a sizable number who have experienced first hand the brutality of dictatorships.

But what we have in common with the readers of the Deuteronomic story of Israel's desire for a king "to rule over us, like the other nations" is not the question of the viability or even desirability of monarchical governance. Israel's historical moment marked the transition and transformation from one form of government, with its attendant cultural and social patterns of living, to a dramatically different way of being and living. While a United States audience would not appear to be on the brink of such a dramatic change, the questions, fears, and temptations that accompanied Israel's decision, with YHWH's blessing, to undertake such a new thing have their parallels in our own experience. Israel's move out of tribal society and into a centralized national monarchy produced culture and faith-relations dynamics unknown before, as Israel became inevitably "like the [other] nations." The constant worry to YHWH and the Prophets in the First Testament is *the consequences* of Israel living as a nation among the nations. The worrisome character of the tension here is caught up in the fact that the Hebrew word for "nations" in our passage (*gôyyîm*) simultaneously indicates those outside the followers of YHWH. To "become like the nations" is to risk losing identity as the people of YHWH. Yet for Israel to remake a tribal society into a national society is the price to be paid for living in competition with the nations.

"For both the church and the civil community, this text at least makes it clear that public questions are central to the Bible. It is difficult but unavoidable to ask, What does the reality of this God authorize and require in terms of public power? In ancient Israel this question evoked a harsh dispute. Very likely every opinion expressed as a conviction of faith was also an assertion of vested interest. The power of vested interest surely is at work in the weighty teaching of Samuel."—Brueggemann, *First and Second Samuel*, Interpretation, 67–68.

This story of the moment of decision for monarchy in Israel pushes upon us the opportunity to reflect upon the consequences of our national commitments—"encumbrances," one writer has called them—in light of our commitment to covenant relationship with God and the practice of Christian discipleship. Reading 1 Samuel 8 allows us to say from a distance what Samuel cannot or does not say in the story: Our commitment is first to God, to whom we belong heart, soul, and mind, and the nature of our social patterns and institutions ought to grow from this prior and encompassing loyalty. We are *both* disciples *and* citizens, neither only one nor the other at any time. That's what makes the constant vigilance required to be good citizens and faithful disciples simultaneously so extraordinarily difficult. As for Israel, so for us the great temptation is to break the tension and, having let it go, fall into idolatry. If we dissolve the tension in favor of discipleship, the temptation is to religious sectarianism or to the practice of a faith disconnected from social and cultural reality. If the tension is relieved, on the other hand, by letting go of discipleship in favor of citizenship, the temptation is to idolatry of the state or to a relativism that ultimately leaves each individual as the measure of what is good and right. Many believe that this cultural relativism was predominant in the 1980s and '90s.

The Reformed traditions have recognized, since John Calvin's efforts in Geneva, the importance and necessity of the church being faithfully engaged in making and re-forming the body politic. Reformed piety calls for the practice of good citizenship that is fundamentally informed by discipleship, that perceives human society as the setting for God's redemptive work for justice and love for all. Citizenship that participates in God's saving love works especially for the poor, for the defenseless, for the stranger, and for the marginalized— those who live on the edge of the society—and the outcast—those excluded because they do not conform to cultural and social mores. Clearly these are not the lobbying interest groups with power to get governance attention, unless the citizen-disciples of Christ make them their cause and lobby from love for justice for them.

These reflections do not mean that 1 Samuel 8 has become a "social action" passage for girding up political loins. What they mean to underscore is just how difficult the practice of living as citizen-disciples is for the followers of Christ, committed as we are to loving God with all our heart, soul, and strength—the entirety of our being—and to loving our neighbor as ourselves. It is not easy for good disciples to be good citizens. But it is necessary. The tension in our commitments leads to ambiguity in countless moments of decision perhaps not as dramatic but every bit as consequential as those facing the elders of Israel before Samuel. What are we, what am I, to do here or there? How shall I vote? How is love served by this or that referendum? On a personal level, how shall we teach patriotism to our children that does not usurp the place of God, to whom we all belong, human and non-human, across the whole earth? How shall we order our lives to reflect justice and love in the places we work, the way we do business, and the pattern of life we establish for family relations and activity? The decisions concerning things like these that we make day after day have Samuel-like consequences in that they form and re-form the direction and content of our ongoing faith story. From here on, as we study Samuel, we will watch to see how the decision at Ramah shaped the future for Samuel, Israel, and YHWH. From here on, we can pay attention to our own decisions about how to live faithfully in the "land," the places and times God has given us, and imagine how they are shaping our future, now.

📖 Want to Know More?

About the Ark of the Covenant? See Werner H. Schmidt, *The Faith of the Old Testament: A History* (Philadelphia: Westminster Press, 1983), 112–16; and Walther Eichrodt, *Theology of the Old Testament*, vol. 1, Old Testament Library (Philadelphia: Westminster Press, 1961), 107–13.

About the period of the judges? See John Bright, *A History of Israel*, 3d ed. (Philadelphia: Westminster Press, 1981), 173–82.

About the concept of God as divine king? See Jerome F. D. Creach, *Psalms*, Interpretation Bible Studies (Louisville, Ky.: Geneva Press, 1998), 48–58.

❓ Questions for Reflection

1. God has seen what happened in the past when the people turned away from God. Why then does God now accede to their wishes for "a king to judge us"? Can't God see the hardships that will follow?
2. The elders gave two reasons for why they wanted a king: (1) Samuel's sons were corrupt, in their view; and (2) They wanted to be "like the other nations." Which of these reasons do you think hurt Samuel the most? Which do you think hurt God the most?
3. Even after talking to God, Samuel is very resistant to the idea of switching from judgeship to kingship. Can you think of a time in

your life when you had a hard time making a change even though you knew it was what God wanted you to do?

4. The constitutional separation of church and state is one aspect of our society that sets our government apart from many others. What does God's approval of, and later involvement in, the naming of a king for God's people say to us today?

3

1 Samuel 12:1–25

Samuel s Farewell Sermon

If you come to this chapter directly from the discussion of chapter 8, the first verse here is a surprise. Samuel's speech to "all Israel" assumes that a kingship is already a "done deal." At the end of chapter 8, Samuel sent everyone home *without* giving them a king, as they asked. But now, it seems, the deed of king-making, which Samuel so resisted earlier, has taken place. Furthermore, the king—Saul—is the one who leads Israel, in place of the prophet-judge Samuel. Making Saul king is the burden of the narrative in chapters 9–11. It is an interesting, if at times bizarre, account of the eventual emergence of Israel's first king. But we can pass over it if we glean some essential matters from these three intervening chapters.

Samuel at Ramah

First of all, taken on the face of it, Saul is said to have become king through two different and unrelated events. In the first (9:1–10:16), Saul becomes king through a secret anointing at the hands of the prophet Samuel. In the second (10:17–27), Samuel convenes the assembly of the people at Mizpah and, after chastising them for their rejection of YHWH as king and recalling the insistence of the people that he give them a king, Saul is identified as the divine choice to become king. "Samuel said to all the people, 'Do you see the one whom the LORD has chosen? There is no one like him among all the people.' And all the people shouted, 'Long live the king!'"(10:24). The Deuteronomic writer of 1 Samuel perhaps knew of more than one account of how Saul became king and has brought them together here, simply laying them side by side to make the single theological claim that YHWH has made the choice of Israel's king. Also, both accounts make the point—important to the Deuteronomist—that Samuel, the last judge and protector of the old traditions of Israel's covenant faith, was a reluctant participant in king-making.

A second matter of interest in chapters 9–11 is the prominence of Samuel and spirit-filled judgeship in the narrative. Samuel, like Eli before him, stands within ancient testimony that God "raised up" leadership to deliver the people of God whenever they were threatened from their enemies. The book of Judges contains accounts of these individual deliverers, who, once the crisis was past, served as "judges" over all the tribes. As we've seen, occupation of the land and fear arising from enemy kingdoms, particularly the encroaching and belligerent Philistines, contributed to growing mistrust of this usual way of doing things. Samuel's reluctance to acquiesce to the popular demand for a king—and thus a new way of governing—carries with it a persistent reaffirmation of the desirability of the judgeship model for Israel's life in the land. If Israel is to have a king, these chapters seem to imply, it must be one who is spirit-filled, as the judges were, and clearly identified for leadership and service by divine choice. In this way, these chapters begin a process toward trying to find a legitimate place within the old traditions of Israel for a king, and we can see that process reach a climax in chapter 12.

> A judge was a person "whom God raised up to lead a revolt against foreign oppressors and who, having freed the nation and shown thereby his [or her] call of God, was looked to by the people to maintain their rights." There were 12 judges: Othniel of Judah, Ehud, Shamgar, Deborah, Gideon, Tola, Jair, Jephthah, Ibzan, Elon, Abdon, and Samson. Eli and Samuel also judged Israel, Eli in his official capacity of high priest and Samuel as a prophet of the Lord.— *The New Westminster Dictionary of the Bible* (Philadelphia: Westminster Press, 1970), 528.

The most graphic place to see this continued commitment to the pattern of "spirit-filled" leadership is 1 Samuel 10:27–11:15. In this story about the victory of Saul over King Nahash and the Ammonites, Saul acts very much like Deborah, Gideon, or Sampson, whose judgeships are narrated in the book of Judges. He sees the distress of the people of Jabesh-gilead, their weeping (11:5) and, upon hearing the terrible thing about to befall them at the hands of Nahash, Saul is "filled with the spirit of God . . . in power, and his anger was greatly kindled (11:6, author's translation). He summons all the tribes together and leads them against Nahash, gaining with God's help a great victory (11:11). In all this, Saul acts much more like judge than king; and, in fact, the closing verse of chapter 11 affirms, "So all the people went to Gilgal, and there they made Saul king before YHWH in Gilgal" (11:15).

The significance of the Deuteronomic Historian's portrayal of Saul's victory under the power of the spirit of God over Nahash is twofold. First, it continues themes we've seen before; it celebrates a saving act from God that raises Saul up as a military leader just in the nick of time. Second, it carries the old traditions of Mosaic covenant and judgeship into the new era of kingship that begins with Saul in chapter 13. The theological bridge between them is formed by chapter 12.

Chapter 12 may be divided into three parts; Samuel is the predominant speaker throughout, and the whole chapter has the form and feel of a sermon (Hertzberg, 97). Three-point sermons are familiar to all of us, and our experience of listening to pastoral "instruction" on a Sunday morning is worth keeping in mind for comparison and contrast as we reflect on the chapter. Like all good preachers, Samuel understands his calling as prophet and judge to include "instructing," literally *torah*-ing Israel in "the good and upright way in which to walk" (see v. 23) within the covenant relationship between the community of faith and YHWH.

> "Chapter 12 is a sermon. . . . The preacher is Samuel, the audience the people of his time." Hertzberg, *I and II Samuel: A Commentary*, 97.

Samuel begins his sermon in a way surprising to most of us as listeners. In fact, we would be distressed if our preacher spent the first few minutes of the sermon asking us, through a series of rhetorical questions, to vindicate his or her behavior over the course of service to the church. Yet that is what Samuel does. Paul writes similarly to the Galatians, vindicating his call to be an apostle (Gal. 1:11–24); and elsewhere he writes to churches in a boasting tone that has typically turned off students in my Sunday school classes, despite his protest that he is "boasting only in Christ."

Let us recognize at the beginning of this discussion that speeches and sermons play a very prominent and important role in the Deuteronomic telling of Israel's story. One of the reasons for this, *literally,* is that speeches afford the best opportunity for the Historian to contribute his own point of view. Speeches, when retold or rewritten, virtually always invite the reteller to modify the original—even in modern situations, where the original may be easy to retrieve. We are all accustomed to reading speeches in our newspapers "the morning after" that are abbreviated or interpreted versions of what we heard the speaker say on television the night before. And some of us who have been speakers marvel at the variations on a theme that limited media space may produce! The point here is not that all speeches in 1 and 2 Samuel, or for that matter the sermons of Moses in Deuteronomy, are "made up" by the Deuteronomic writer, and therefore we are free to dismiss them as inauthentic. Rather, it is that speeches and sermons afford the Deuteronomic Historian, who is concerned above all with providing a history that can inform the identity of the community of faith, with the best place to sum up and interpret events. These creative spaces, at the same time, in many subtle ways provide readers—ancient and modern—with clues to the meaning of the whole narrative history.

To return to Samuel's opening statements (vv. 1–5), the sermon is presented as his farewell address to all Israel. As in chapter 8, we are reminded of his old age; however, he will not die until he has served as the instrument of judgment against the king he has just anointed and has anointed David to rule instead. Amazingly, his death is not noted in the narrative until 1 Samuel 28:3. That makes us wonder why Samuel's "farewell," as many scholars have called this chapter, is here and not closer to chapter 28. What purpose does it serve here in the narrative? In this location, Samuel's sermon serves as his "farewell" to the role he has played on Israel's behalf as judge; he will continue to serve as prophetic critic to the king, but judgeship in Israel ends here. And thus the importance of Samuel's desire that the people "bear witness" to the way in which he has conducted himself as judge over Israel during his long tenure. The congregation affirms Samuel's righteousness; that is, his uprightness with regard to the way he has conducted himself as judge. By so doing, subtly but surely, the viability and reliability of judgeship is also affirmed—a point of theological importance to the Deuteronomic Historian, who knows the tragic route down which kingship will eventually lead Israel.

Walter Brueggemann makes the insightful point that Samuel's speech about his own conduct represents the "flip side" of the behavior of kings against which he warned in chapter 8 (Brueggemann, 90). The key to this comparison is in the frequent use of "take" in both speeches. With reference to kings, you may recall, Samuel warned against their tendency to "take, take, take" from the people (8:11–17, the verb being used 5 times). But in 12:1–5 Samuel testifies, and the people confirm as true, that he did not "take, take" (3 times in v. 3 and once in v. 4). The implication from this contrast between Samuel and the coming kings is instructive for us: Good leadership is characterized not by "taking" but by service, by carrying out one's duty responsibly and without causing oppression and suffering among the people. These concepts, along with their twins, defrauding and stealing, have bundles of both literal and metaphorical meanings worth our reflecting upon.

Samuel, as a publicly confirmed righteous judge whose good character and behavior lend power and authority to his sermon, is now set to require Israel to do as he has done: to "take your stand, that I may judge you before YHWH" (v. 7, author's translation). As the people stood as witnesses before God to affirm Samuel's righteousness as judge, now they stand before Samuel, the judge, and before YHWH, who remarkably is called as witness in this trial of the character and behavior of the people of God (v. 6). The body of Samuel's sermon (vv. 6–17) is a judgment speech against the people who have just added to their sin with their demand for the king they have just acclaimed. It reflects the pattern of other prophetic judgment speeches in the First Testament, which includes a recitation of the "righteousnesses of YHWH," usually translated as God's "saving deeds" (v. 7). The awkwardness of my more literal translation, "righteousnesses," serves a purpose. "Righteousness" is a relational term in the Bible; it is not first and foremost about keeping rules. Rather, it is first and foremost about staying in "right relationship" with God and with our neighbor. It is a word that defines the covenant relationship between YHWH and YHWH's chosen people. We are righteous people not because we always do right—which we don't (see the famous confession from Paul in Romans 7)—but because we may stand in "right relationship" with YHWH and others whom YHWH loves.

So Samuel lays forth the story of YHWH's "righteousnesses" toward the people who were formed by the delivering actions of a God who cannot stand to hear the cry of oppressed persons. The story tells of YHWH's repeated efforts to set Israel free to become God's people and enjoy the life of fullness and peace that such a relationship brings. It also tells of the community's repeated betrayal of their covenant relationship with YHWH, how they forsook YHWH in favor of "following after the Ba'alim and the 'Ashtaroth"—collective

30

names for idols of all sorts. Amazingly, in each case, though YHWH hands them over to their enemies for judgment for their apostasy, when they cry out from oppression again YHWH delivers them, restores them, and renews the covenant. The dominant actions that describe the behavior of the people across the history of their covenant relationship with God, in the vocabulary of the Deuteronomic Historian, are "forget," "forsake," and "follow after idols." Those describing YHWH's activity include "heard their cry," "delivered" or "rescued," and "gave." This is not to dismiss the testimony that YHWH is said to have "sold" the people into the hands of their enemies as punishment for their covenant-breaking. Nevertheless, the bottom line for the Historian-theologian is Samuel's statement that the people of God need not fear, for "YHWH will not cast away" (v. 22) those who have been freed to live joyfully within the covenant relationship with one another and with God. That's good news for those in exile in the 6th century B.C.E. when the Historian created our narrative. It is very good news for us now, as well.

Much has been said about what has appeared to many Christians over the years as the harshness of the pattern of divine retribution that plays throughout the Deuteronomic writing. The blessing-curse balance, vividly displayed in Deuteronomy 28:1–68, may seem to many to lack the generosity of love we associate with God in Christ. To be sure, this "if you do right—this; if you do wrong—that" perspective on justice can be and has been hardened into a mechanistic theology. Such a view reads situational evidence backwards to conclude that since one is wealthy, one must be blessed; or since one is suffering loss, one must have done something wrong to deserve it. Job's friends' poor counsel to the suffering Job dramatically represents this frozen thinking. But the spirit of this kind of thinking is well represented in our own day. In businesses and in congregations, it is visible in a perspective that assumes that if business is not booming, it is failing; or if the church is not growing, it is because our ministry is not as blessed as another church's. Addressing the critical problems of this kind of theological reasoning is too big a task to tackle here. It is a complicated issue, but it is as near to each of us as our questions about "why, God" that tearfully flow from every tragedy we experience or about which we learn.

Samuel's sermon, with its patented recounting of the "righteousnesses of YHWH" and the "unrighteousnesses" of the people of God, offers more insight regarding this so-called pattern of retributive justice in the First Testament than may first meet the eye. First, note where the community's sacred story begins. It recalls first the deliverance from oppression for a people who had no identity by a God whose identity was cloaked in a mysterious affirmation to the one raised up to facilitate the deliverance. (See Exodus 3:14, where the Holy Name is translated variously "I will be who I will be" or "I am who I am" or "I will cause to happen what happens.") Whatever the translation, the meaning is reflected in YHWH's intent to empower Moses to compel Pharaoh to "let my people go." That is, it is a name for defining a relationship with a people who are to be set free, given a place to live in peace and a purpose for which to live, and fulfilled in wholehearted and faithful service of YHWH and love of others. We are not talking about "retributive justice" in the abstract then. We are talking about appropriate behavior and justice *within the covenant* initiated by God to save strangers and oppressed persons and make them into a community with an identity bound to the memory of their being set free for God's purposes.

The covenant, from the beginning, set down certain expectations both of God and of the people of God. "I will be your God; you will be my people." To that a grateful people at once pledged allegiance. YHWH's promise included protection against enemies, guidance, and generally seeing to the welfare of God's people. The people, for their part, pledged to keep God's Word and to obey God's commandments, chief among which, from the Deuteronomic point of view, was the First Commandment, requiring absolute and unwavering loyalty and service to YHWH. What happens, though, when the covenant promise is broken by the people, as we are all likely to do? "Absolute and unwavering loyalty" is a very high bar to set, though surely not an inappropriate response to the God who has given us life. The answer is "grace." Grace happens. That is, YHWH single-handedly ("with an outstretched hand" is the biblical image) heals the broken relationship and restores the covenant promises—something no covenanting deity is required to do.

Where does punishment come in? It is for the Historian a pedagogical tool.

> "In our conventional perception of our social world, we may let the king and all the other players in the game of Realpolitik loom too large. We may give more credit and attention to such actors than is warranted. If so, this is a wondrous chapter for putting historical reality back into covenantal perspective. Chapter 12 asserts without reservation that there is another governance that merits and must have more of our attention."—Brueggemann, *First and Second Samuel,* Interpretation, 96.

Handing the people over to their enemies demonstrates the worthlessness and powerlessness of the gods for whom the people abandoned the covenant with YHWH. Furthermore, it hopefully leads to the confession of betrayal that allows for genuine forgiveness and restoration to take place. Forgiveness that comes too easily fails to take the necessity of repentance seriously and to require evidence of real change before relationships can be truly restored. So YHWH tutors a straying people. We are, after all, "frequent flyers" after relationships that are easy and undemanding, after the tempting habit of defining our own right and wrong and making gods of things that will not really make us happy or save us from the dangers and fears we seek to escape. If we will listen to and obey the voice of God— and that voice only—God will keep us within God's loving embrace. But if we push away, there is no way God can hold us against our will. Nevertheless, we are never—even when turning a deaf ear to God— cast aside: that is the Deuteronomic theology, and it far exceeds the cold calculations of "retributive justice."

Brueggemann concludes by saying that the chapter "intends to renew in ancient Israel a moral vision of the historical process when the moral vision was skewed by fear, calculation, and vested interest" (Brueggemann, 96). He then points to our own need to renew a moral vision that attends to the narrative of our own times. This sense of our national need for a renewal of a moral vision by which to live is widespread, judging from newspaper and television articles and interviews and the outpouring of books on "family values" and arguments for moral education in our homes and our schools. To be sure, not all those who champion a renewed morality these days agree on what that means. If you ask, "What do you think are the key moral values by which persons need to live to be happy and whole?" to members of a study group gathered around this book, for instance, I promise you a lively and diverse discussion. The results of in-depth interviews with Protestant baby-boomers about faith and belief, published in *Vanishing Boundaries: The Religion of Mainline Protestant Baby Boomers* (1994), are apropos. While parents may be unclear about their beliefs and talk about them little, the study showed that beliefs matter and that parents want religious education for their children, especially around moral instruction and the inculcation of a moral code like the Ten Commandments. Boomers believe, according to the authors' research, that a shared moral code of conduct is necessary to "the good life" (Hoge et al., 111).

Stephen Carter, author of *Integrity* (1996), recounts how, as he was beginning work on his book on the virtue of integrity, he began a commencement address by announcing that his topic was integrity.

33

The audience responded with spontaneous and enthusiastic applause, though they had not yet heard a single word of his speech (Carter, 5). Carter's fine book is an in-depth exploration of the meaning of integrity, which he defines in a way that sets the bar too high for most of us to succeed at being what he calls an "integral person" all of the time. We have already suggested that the covenant standards of YHWH, which for the Christian are expressed in the two-sided commandment of Jesus that we love God with our whole being and our neighbor as ourselves, are equally out of reach for us in every instance of our lives as disciples. Though thoroughly sensitive to religious aspects of integrity, Carter is writing for what he calls an "unfortunately secular" society. Still, his understanding of the "three steps" necessary for an "integral life" as a good citizen (Carter, 9–10) has value for our reflection on what a "faithful life" as a good disciple may require. Quickly, and oversimply, Carter's steps are these: the integral person must routinely (1) discern carefully right from wrong; (2) act upon the results of his or her discernment; and (3) articulate what he or she believes is right and wrong and what action properly follows from it.

Want to Know More?

About *torah*? See Jerome F. D. Creach, *Psalms*, Interpretation Bible Studies (Louisville, Ky.: Geneva Press, 1998), 22–29.

About the exodus? See James D. Newsome, *Exodus*, Interpretation Bible Studies (Louisville, Ky.: Geneva Press, 1998).

About other gods in ancient times? See Robert M. Grant, *Gods and the One God*, Library of Early Christianity (Philadelphia: Westminster Press, 1986), 19–71.

For the Christian disciple who is committed without reserve to the will of God—the first character principle Samuel sets forth in our chapter for practitioners of covenant faith—discernment of God's will is prior to discerning right from wrong. In fact, it may be the same thing, though I can imagine times when knowing the will of God does not solve the dilemma of knowing the right thing to do in a particular situation. 1 Samuel 12 suggests we have grounds for discerning God's will in the delivering and forming story of the community of God's people, which Christians see continuing in the story of God's incarnation in Christ. Morality for us begins and ends with the "saving righteousnesses" of YHWH: at the Red (or Reed) Sea, in the desert, in the land, in exile, under oppression, in a stable, at the table, on the cross, before an empty tomb, and far beyond even to our own day. How shall we do right and avoid wrong? Or, in Samuel's terms, how shall we walk in "the good and right way"? We do not answer first from a code but with a story of saving grace, within the context of which duties and obligations bind us as acts of thanksgiving and praise.

With Carter, we can affirm, as Samuel does, that covenant faith requires that we walk the walk as well as talk the talk. To listen to sermons or study the Bible to discern the will of God only then to "sit on our hands" in our pews, offices, schools, or homes is a kind of infidelity—perhaps the worst kind, because it is infidelity pretending to be faithfulness. Covenant faith also requires us, as Samuel's story makes clear, to do more. The "more" is the risky business described by Carter's third step. Samuel's sermon is devastatingly critical of the covenant people, and his bold move to subsume kingship to the old traditions of Moses—demanding equal and unqualified loyalty and fidelity from everyone, including "your king"—risked public dismissal like that which he experienced with the elders in chapter 8. Standing up for what we believe, having grounded our conclusions about right and wrong in our faith, is incomplete without being willing and able to articulate the moral choices we advocate in the public square, as well as at home and in church. 1 Samuel 12 offers us a harvest of clues to what we might call "covenant character formation," clues that, upon reflection, can perhaps begin to renew a moral vision for our own time.

 ## Questions for Reflection

1. Why do you think Samuel felt the need to have his righteousness affirmed by the people? Was it insecurity, boasting, or did he have another motive?
2. Have you ever been in a situation where someone asked you to affirm their righteousness? Did it make you feel uncomfortable? How did you respond?
3. What's the difference between "doing right" and being in "right relationship" with God?
4. Discuss ways that the divine retribution that occurs in some Old Testament writings has harmed our society's view of "blessings and curses."

4

1 Samuel 15:1–35

Royal Sin
and Disastrous Consequences

No chapter we've studied so far gives Christian readers a wrenching pause like 1 Samuel 15. The stories about Saul's kingship in chapters 13 and 14, while leading us here, cannot prepare us for the test of obedience that YHWH lays upon Saul and the people of God with the unequivocal command to blot out the Amalekites, sparing no one and nothing that belongs to them. The drama that unfolds in the narrative of this chapter involves the narrator sparsely; the bulk of these 35 verses portrays YHWH, Samuel, and Saul locked in a dynamic process of royal self-destruction.

I vividly remember exploring this chapter with our Sunday school class. When we finished reading the text out loud, there were a few minutes of stunned silence. It was the kind of slack-jawed, speechless moment many of us experienced recently as witnesses to the tragic deaths of John F. Kennedy Jr., his wife, and her sister en route to a family wedding. The commentators all asked our whispered question: "How much loss can this star-crossed Kennedy family take?" With the death of President John F. Kennedy in 1963, the hope of a generation not yet grown cynical that the promise of a national re-creation was within reach was severely shaken. Then, in 1968, Robert Kennedy was assassinated just two months after Martin Luther King Jr., and the hope of a stunned nation was crushed again. Now, in 1999, death strikes once more at the Kennedys' heart, which has become over these three decades something of a national heart, too. "Why?" we all wonder in grief. Why would God seem to call out this family for public service and then permit (cause?) their destruction one by one? The commentators and even the family reminded us on each occasion: "Life goes on." But tragedy like this that spans generations like a Greek play leaves us uncomprehendingly silent, begging to know just how to live if life just "goes on" and if God's place in it is as devastating and chaotic as it seems.

If the Deuteronomic writer's intention was for readers to find Saul's behavior reprehensible and nod understandingly at the uncompromising judgment against him (vv. 26, 28), that certainly did not happen in our class. Quite the opposite: our sympathy almost universally reached out to Saul and our revulsion was reserved for YHWH and the prophet Samuel. Frankly, to many, Saul's "sparing" of Agag and some of the "spoil" of the Amalekites, as the text describes it, seemed far more ethically laudable than YHWH's order to kill them all and destroy everything that belonged to them. Yet such a conclusion was uncomfortable for us and very hard to admit: Accusing God of uncompromising slaughter of human beings, Amalekites or not, seems to border on unfaithfulness at best and heresy at worst. So we dug in, as you are doing, to face the question that generations before us have faced. What shall we do with this chapter that seems to portray God-initiated violence against people and their possessions without mercy, that seems, frankly, so far removed from St. John's affirmation that "God is love."

> The Amalekites were descendants of Esau who harassed the Israelites and engaged with them in battle from time to time. In Saul's time their bands roamed through a stretch of 500 to 600 miles of wilderness from the border of Egypt to Havilah (northern central Arabia). After a crushing defeat by Saul and another by David, the Amalekites that remained were destroyed by the sons of Simeon during the reign of Hezekiah.—See *The New Westminster Dictionary of the Bible* (Philadelphia: Westminster Press, 1970), 34

One apparent option needs facing up front. We might choose to ignore the chapter, deciding on a first reading that there is no "word from God" here for us as Christians in the contemporary world. The Bible necessarily bears the marks of the cultures and societies over a long period of time that gave it its language, imagery, social patterns, and ethical frameworks. That is part of its glory and richness. However, not all of these features translate well in every case into the patterns and ethos of a modern political culture or into the expressions of modern languages. The difficulty, for example, of hearing God's Word for us through words rooted and shaped in ancient patriarchal societies is well known; and feminist scholars have worked hard to help us interpret the Bible in ways that break the bonds of biblical patriarchy. The point is that one could declare 1 Samuel 15, with its slaughter of an enemy, to be so contrary to our understanding of human rights, the defensible conduct of war, and a merciful, loving

God that there can be no word from God for us here. Rather, there can be only words that alienate us from God or obscure the true character of God as we know God in Christ.

But this conclusion absolutely must await a far more careful examination of the narrative than a first reading permits or than our impulse to defend God's loving image allows. There is much at stake here, including two fundamental principles of Reformed approaches to the Bible. One principle concerns the *wholeness* of the Bible and the refusal of the Reformers, most ardently John Calvin, to allow a *supersessionist* approach to biblical interpretation. Such a view would argue that the Second (or New) Testament supersedes theologically the First (or Old) Testament, meaning that the First Testament is, effectively, a "second-class citizen" when it comes to revealing a Word from God. Put differently and looking at a text like 1 Samuel 15, one might take one look and conclude that the mercy that Jesus taught makes null, if not void, the story of God's rejection of Saul over his refusal to commit mayhem as ordered. Indeed, Jesus' teaching that God desires mercy more than sacrifice (Matt. 9:13; 12:7; Mark 12:33) is a striking contrast to Samuel's declaration to Saul that God desires obedience more than sacrifice (15:22). But to read chapter 15 from a point of view that sees the First Testament as effectively replaced by the Second in terms of authority for Christian life violates the Reformed insistence that the Bible is, in its entirety, the Word of God written. Such a reading prematurely chokes our chapter of its possible meaning for us.

The second principle of Reformed interpretation that is at stake is the conviction that biblical words become a Word from God through the power of the Holy Spirit at work in the community of interpreters which is the church. "Community of interpreters" describes well a Bible study group or a Sunday school class. It may also describe individuals in their efforts to interpret the Bible as they read and, as such, reminds individuals that each of us interprets within the community of faith. That binds us to seek the Holy Spirit in our reading and reflecting together or alone, and it binds us to seek the wisdom of the church's traditions and contemporary scholars and commentators. God promises to help us find the meaning for our lives in even the most difficult Bible passages, if we will be open to the Spirit and have within ourselves what Calvin called "a teachable spirit."

Brueggemann provides us with a clue for reading 1 Samuel 15 when he locates the chapter in the context of the sequence of the narrative from 1 Samuel 9–15. He says, "Chapters 13–15 form something of a counterpoint to chapters 9–11. In chapters 9–11 we have seen how Saul was established as king. . . . Now in chapters 13–15 we . . . observe the undoing of Saul and the end of his royal power" (Brueggemann, 97). At the center of this point-counterpoint stands chapter 12, the subject of our last session. The clue that emerges for us here concerns the purpose for which the narrative was composed.

Ancient readers of this narrative faced three questions to which chapter 15 seems to respond. First, the overarching question: how will the new form of governance fare in Israel. The writer's conviction that Israel's fatal sin could be traced to their demand for a king and the consequent rejection of the sovereignty of YHWH we have seen prefigured in chapters 8 and 12. Nevertheless, we, the readers, must follow the writer's setting forth this history bit by bit until, at the end, as the writer hopes, we will draw the same conclusion as he. Saul is the first king, and ancient readers watched in chapters 13–15, as we do, the story of the monarchy unfold against this larger Deuteronomic backdrop.

The second question before the ancient audience following this history concerned Saul personally. If we are following the story line, we wonder, too. How will he do? What will he do as king? Can the hopes of the Elders that led to the demand for a king be fulfilled in Saul? Can he lead Israel successfully into battle against its formidable opponents, the Philistines, and guard the emerging nation from other threats? Will he listen to YHWH's word and do it, as charged by the prophet Samuel in the ceremony at Gilgal? Will he prove to be the obedient anointed one, following after YHWH and not forsaking YHWH for other gods? All these questions hang in the air after chapter 12, but they are collectively focusing on the loyalty and competency of Saul as king.

The third question playing throughout the Saul narrative for ancient readers and for us concerns needed explanation for a well-known fact. Part of the stability Israel sought in asking for a king rested in the assumption of legitimate succession within the institution, rather than depending on a leader to arise when a national crisis or even a crisis for one tribe threatened. How then, historically, may it be explained that Saul was replaced as king by David, someone not of his family and, indeed, not even of his own tribe?

Between the lines of these ancient questions are deeper issues about power and politics, the sovereignty of God, obedience and betrayal, fidelity and compromise. These are lessons the Deuteronomic writer wishes to teach the ancient audience, and they are issues still vital to us and our practice of Christian faith. The writer whose history we are reading, as I noted in an earlier unit, uses his recollection of events in Israel's life to help his people form their identity, to help them know who they are by seeing the way that has led them to their present. Identity questions, then, guide the history's unfolding. They may guide our search for meaning for us, too. We may keep this in mind as we look at the details of chapter 15.

"Surely, to obey is better than sacrifice."
—1 Sam. 15:22

The chapter might well be called "the testing of Saul." It has about it a feel not unlike Genesis 22, the sacrifice of Isaac, in which Abraham and Sarah's faith is tested in the extreme. Or think of Exodus 32 (with its parallel in Deuteronomy 9) and the testing of Aaron, placed in charge while Moses was on the mountain with God receiving the commandments. Aaron failed his test and blamed the people for his disobedience, in a move paralleled in Saul's story. Finally, consider the powerful temptation of Jesus to avoid a horrible death on the cross. The scene in Gethsemane, emblazoned in our minds and hearts, makes it clear that Jesus found the road leading to his own death hard to take; but agonizing prayer led him to the conclusion that God's will required it (see Matt. 26:36–46; Luke 22:39–46).

Each of these stories, like 1 Samuel 15, involves a test of wills—human will and divine will in profound confrontation. Faith affirms that God wills what is good for human beings and all creation; and indeed the community of faith is called to do God's good, to be "a blessing" to the earth. Yet biblical stories of testing times confirm our own experience that it is sometimes very difficult to see the good of God's will in particular situations. Nevertheless, these stories, like 1 Samuel 15, focus tightly on the question concerning whether or not those who have pledged their fidelity to YHWH can keep *their* word and, in the face of great challenge, actually *do* the will of God as revealed to them. As readers, then, the nature of the test adds to the power of the drama and the depth of the challenge to the human will. The conviction of the biblical writers is that the human will is inclined to follow its own path rather than to follow God. That's what it means to say we are sinful or given to sin. The testing stories say, "Let's just see this time." The essential point here is this: The events that constitute the opportunity for testing are not the issue; what is at stake is quite clearly whether or not the persons involved in the events prove faithful to their promise to keep YHWH's word and not turn away from doing it.

The word that rings throughout chapter 15 confirms the point. "Hear" is the dominating summons of the narrative, the word *shema'* occurring seven times. The summons to "hear" is simultaneously a summons to "do," to "obey," to respond completely to what is heard. The test of Saul dramatized in this chapter is about his ability to "hear/do" what is required of him as the one whom God has chosen to be king over Israel. For the historian, the Amalekites are not the issue; Saul's obedience is.

On the other hand, the fact that the mission on which Saul is sent by the prophet Samuel aims at the total destruction of the Amalekites is not incidental to the historian's narrative. Saul's test recalls the last command set forth by Moses before Israel entered the land, according to Deuteronomy 25:17–19. Our writer connects the command in Deuteronomy with the story of Saul's test as king. The conditions are right, as Deuteronomy anticipated them: Israel is now settled in the land and, for the moment at least, its enemies have been subdued. Now is the opening Deuteronomy anticipated, the right time for the campaign against the hated Amalekites. The harshness of the judgment against the Amalekites gains perspective from the Deuteronomic connection, too. Because of their crimes against the entering tribes, their memory is to be blotted from the land. Thus the land is to be purged of their sin. For that reason, the writer describes the campaign as *herem,* a holy war in which nothing is to be gained or taken as booty and all is to be treated as "devoted" or sacrificed to God. All this provides the story of Saul with a context that, from the writer's point of view, is fully commensurate with his role as Israel's first king. He is to be tested on the battlefield, as one would expect of any king; but this field of battle is also an altar upon which the chosen one of YHWH is expected to carry out the whole-offering holy war requires.

As Saul's trial—the language and form *is* juridical (see Brueggemann, 113)—unfolds in verses 10–31, the writer invites us into the midst of it. The word to Saul was to slay all the Amalekites and he seems convinced that he has kept YHWH's word (v. 13). The reader knows even before this verse, however, that Agag, the king, and the choicest of the livestock have been spared; and so far Saul has given no explanation for this compromise of the word of YHWH. YHWH, on the other hand, offers no doubt: Verse 10 is a devastating word of judgment that pronounces the rejection of Saul as king by the very One who chose him.

Our sympathies, I suspect, tend to run with Saul at this point. Suppose we can set aside the horror that the whole spectacle of a holy war may raise in our modern conscience. We remain stunned by the sharp and unyielding judgment that YHWH pronounces on him for what is, at worst, only a *partial* failure to carry out the divine orders. The language is shocking: YHWH declares: "I repent that I made Saul king, for he has turned away from following me and my word he has not carried out" (v. 10, author's translation). The NRSV's translation "I regret," while perhaps more idiomatic in English, loses the power of the Hebrew verb when it is used with God as its subject. Here is admission of a divine mistake. Not just regret is expressed, but a kind of confession—"I was wrong to make Saul king." YHWH's repenting leaves no doubt: There is no room for Saul to find a way back into the role of chosen king of Israel. With this pronouncement, Saul's authority and power as king cease, even though he will remain in office for some time to come.

> "Samuel's initial speech sounds like a legal process (vv. 17–19). It consists of three elements. The first element is a reminder to Saul that he is in fact a nobody. . . . The second element reiterates the commission of verses 2–3 (v. 18). . . . Third, there is an indictment with three questions (v. 19)."—Brueggemann, *First and Second Samuel*, Interpretation, 113.

Saul's explanation for sparing Agag and the livestock of the Amalekites seems to us plausible. They brought them to Gilgal, Saul tells Samuel, to sacrifice them at this sanctuary to YHWH. Moreover, the people wanted it so; they are the ones who did not carry out the slaughter in the valley of the Amalekites. Samuel, who delivers YHWH's harsh judgment to Saul, is not buying the excuse; and clearly God is not either. Samuel's speech (v. 19) offers a telling difference with Saul's claim of innocence in verse 15. Samuel asks Saul, "Why did you not listen to the voice of YHWH, instead of *swooping down* upon the spoil and doing evil in the sight of YHWH?" The implication of the verb here is that Saul and his army acted with greed, taking the spoil not to sacrifice but for their own profit. Therein lies Saul's great sin: not only does he fail to do the word of

YHWH, but allows what was to be devoted to YHWH to become wealth for the people who claimed the livestock for themselves. The motivation for disobedience, as Samuel apparently sees it, is not the impossibility of the task but the greed of those under Saul's command, if not Saul himself. At the end of a judgment speech that begins in verse 22, Samuel dramatically declares the consequences of Saul's disobedience, rejecting at the same time the proffered justification that the king and people meant all along to sacrifice the spoil. "Because you have forsaken

> "In the end we are left with the harsh verdict on Saul: 'reject,' Such a verdict, however justified, brings with it deep grief. That is where Saul's tale ends, not in hostility or in anger but in grief, for both Samuel and perhaps for Yahweh (v. 35)."—Brueggemann, *First and Second Samuel,* Interpretation, 118.

the word of YHWH, YHWH has forsaken you as king" (v. 23). What could be more devastating for Saul, apart from losing his life, than being forsaken by YHWH as king? Once again, he is the "nobody" he was before he was the chosen and anointed king of all Israel. Politically, he will continue as king until David assumes the rule in the future; but he will rule without YHWH, which is illegitimate, dangerous, and ultimately self-destructive, as the narrative will soon show us.

We turn to ask, "Where are we in this story? How may this chapter shed light on our Christian practices of faith?" We cannot avoid the questions it asks us pointedly.

- What kind of obedience do we render to God? Knowing God's will for the way we live, do we do it?

- What options and alternatives that arise along our path of following God invite us to "fudge" on the lengths to which we are prepared to go to love God with our whole being and our neighbor as ourself?

- When we look at the image of God incarnate in Christ, what excuses do we make for ourselves to justify a different image for our own lives?

These are questions chapter 15's portrayal of YHWH's demand for radical obedience raise for us, not because we are kings, like Saul, but because we are chosen, like Saul, to serve God wholeheartedly.

It is important to say here that the lesson of chapter 15 is *not* that anyone who fails to hear and do the will of God in a single situation is rejected and forsaken by God. As I've said, the drama of chapter 15, in addition to its role as an explanation for how Saul lost the kingship and David became king instead, provides a sharp vignette on the everpresent temptation to do what seems best in one's own eyes and what serves one's own needs rather than the harder work of keeping faith with the Word of God as revealed to us. The consequences of disobedience, make no mistake, are dire. Apart from listening for God's guidance and doing what is required of us, life as God intends it for us cannot be enjoyed. For it turns out, happily, that doing God's will is not only good for God but also good for us, the source of deep meaning, happiness, and hope in life.

Professor Brueggemann suggests that there is another issue that confronts us from this story. He writes, "The narrative invites us to ponder the interface of power and ideology, the requirement of political realism, and the demand for ideological purity" (Brueggemann, 117). Brueggemann's question is a good one for reflection, particularly given the public presence always of one or more groups that approach complex problems from an ideologically set perspective that allows virtually no room for compromise. For example, some Christian groups argue that governing bodies in our public life ought to be guided by Christian principles and values, and thus it is a Christian's responsibility to vote for candidates committed to those values. Saul's story, of course, takes place within a community circumscribed by the law or *Torah* of God. Our circumstances are dramatically different; we live with a Constitutional commitment that no religious body may be favored or established in our governance. The question Brueggemann sees posed to us from this chapter, then, is this: How can those who are called to "listen and obey" the Word of God work and participate in public

---

Want to Know More?

About biblical hermeneutics or interpretation? See Walter Brueggemann, *The Bible Makes Sense* (Atlanta: John Knox Press, 1977) or Paul J. Achtemeier, *The Inspiration of Scripture: Problems and Proposals* (Philadelphia: Westminster Press, 1980).

About God testing us? See Celia Brewer Marshall, *Genesis,* Interpretation Bible Studies (Louisville, Ky.: Geneva Press, 1999), 57–65.

About Holy War? See Werner H. Schmidt, *The Faith of the Old Testament: A History* (Philadelphia: Westminster Press, 1983), 96–100.

About YHWH regretting a decision? See Terence E. Fretheim, *Exodus,* Interpretation (Louisville, Ky.: John Knox Press, 1991), 286–87; for a detailed discussion of the Old Testament presentation of humanlike attributes of God (including changing God's mind), see Horst Dietrich Preuss, *Old Testament Theology,* vol. 1, Old Testament Library (Louisville, Ky.: Westminster John Knox Press, 1995), 244–49.

life, a marketplace of ideas and alternative values, without being compelled to compromise their religious ideals? To put it differently, can any one or any group committed fully to "obedience to God" exercise authority—whether in government or corporate life—fairly and justly without qualifying their ideal of absolute obedience to God?

Let's return for a moment to the "sounds of silence" that reverberated in my Sunday school classroom at the reading of this story and the wider national mumbling in the face of the unspeakable losses suffered by the Kennedy family and, through them, the national spirit. It is clear on reflection that what we have a choice about in such moments is how we respond. Do we sit slack-jawed? Do we offer platitudes to salve seriously wounded hopes and dreams? Or do we continue to live by faith alone—not blindly but in the light of God's radical promises and the radiance of a risen Lord?

Chapter 15 is rich with potential meaning for all of us. Whether you choose to pursue the questions it raises for you in terms of your personal struggles with doing God's will or on the larger horizon of public power and wholehearted commitment to Christian values, a challenging conversation promises to be the outcome. Hopefully, one outcome may be a renewed commitment, more fully understood, to listen to and do what God requires of us and what is, simultaneously, good for us. If so, celebrate it!

 ## Questions for Reflection

1. When you read a passage like this, with its portrayal of YHWH as a violent God who "takes no prisoners," is it your first inclination to skip over it, telling yourself that "God isn't really like that"? Does skipping over it do a disservice to the Bible, and also to God? If so, how?

2. Do you sympathize with Saul while reading this passage? Do you think he repented of his sin (1 Sam. 15:24, 30) more because he was truly sorry for not obeying God or because God had rejected him as king?

3. What kind of obedience do *we* render to God? Knowing God's will for the way we live, do we do it?

4. How can we work in the world—whether it be government or business or academia—without qualifying the ideal of absolute obedience to God?

5 1 Samuel 16:1–13

"Arise, Anoint Him; for This Is He"

We have come at last to the story to which the Deuteronomic writer has been drawing us ever since Hannah's Song in chapter 2: the anointing of David as king over all Israel. On the heels of chapter 15's account of YHWH's angry and absolute rejection of Saul as king, the sunshine of 1 Samuel 16:1–13 is a welcome contrast to the dark clouds hanging over Israel's future when the narrative concluded. Chapter 16 begins where chapter 15 left off, picking up the thread of Samuel's grief over Saul's rejection and YHWH's sorrow ("repentance," literally) over the choice of Saul to be king.

In the opening verse of our chapter, YHWH appears ready to move on with the future of Israel. The judgment announced in chapter 15 is repeated here verbatim: "For I have rejected Saul as ruler over all Israel" (16:1, author's translation). The form of the clause in Hebrew is unmistakably emphatic, and might be literally rendered "I myself have rejected him." Why then, YHWH asks Samuel, do you continue to grieve? If the Holy One, whose heart has been broken by Saul's betrayal, is able to move on, should not Samuel, whose pain could not possibly be as deep, be prepared to take the next steps toward replacing the rejected king? In our English versions, this dynamic between God and God's prophet does not come through to us readily. Some with whom I have studied this passage, in fact, have seen YHWH's words as a rebuke to Samuel. But I think YHWH's shove of Samuel is more a matter of urgency than chastisement. And we miss something very important if we fail to see the divine suffering over Saul that is implied here.

I say it is very important because it is so germane to us who are trying to live faithfully as followers of Christ. Part of what leaves us uneasy about our relationship to God at the end of chapter 15 is wondering about God's radical rejection of Saul for what may appear to us as a minor slip in obedience to God's will. Saul completed God's word at least 90 percent, did he not? How then can YHWH find such fault and take such drastic steps against him? And, if this is a mirror of how God responds to those who fail to give 100 percent obedience to the incredibly wide-sweeping law of Christ, calling us to "love others as we have been loved [by God in Christ]," what possibly can be our relationship with God when clearly we cannot perform love so flawlessly?

What we need to know is given to us in this brief but poignant opening verse in chapter 16. God bypasses calculations of obedience. There can only be, after all, either obedience or disobedience. Something in-between still implies that something other than God's intentions has seduced our loyalty. Recognition of our disobedience, prayers for forgiveness, and a new life that truly reflects repentance, we learned in chapter 12, is the way back into relationship with God. Saul's effort at repentance was meager despite the fact that, as king, given both his privilege and duty, his obedience provided a critically important witness of faith to the people of God, as we discovered in chapters 8 and 12.

We know the same impulse that demands a better, even flawless, moral character from leaders to whom power is entrusted. During the investigations into alleged wrongdoing by President William Clinton and the subsequent impeachment proceedings in Congress, media reports of comments from elected officials and ordinary citizens reflected the feeling that a president should have a more excellent character. A president, it was contended, should be able to be trusted to tell the truth and to be free from sexual or political improprieties. Other citizens countered that such high demand on a human being, *precisely because he or she has been given great power,* is naive. Great power leaves one vulnerable to greater temptations, therefore improprieties in elected office may be regrettable and even reprehensible but nevertheless very understandable, given the human condition.

Let us now return to Saul's conviction by YHWH of wrongdoing, his divine impeachment and removal from office, and our resulting unease regarding ourselves. The verse in chapter 16 at which we are looking reminds us that, beyond any "score keeping," God suffers deeply the breach in relationship that occurs with our disobedience but is nonetheless ready and able to look to a hopeful future in which covenant relationship is restored and betrayal redeemed. God's willingness—even eagerness—to reconnect with us when our love fails to be unconditional toward God or neighbor is remarkably good news for us. God rejected Saul as king, a role that cannot possibly countenance disobedience, no matter the "little bit" left undone or done against God's will. But God did not reject Saul as one of the people of God. How Saul handles his removal as king and return to ordinary life as one of God's people, of course, is up to Saul, not God. And as readers of chapters beyond 16 will learn, those choices proved difficult and ultimately self-destructive for Saul, much, one may safely imagine, to the sorrow of YHWH.

We have been waiting for David, but the narrator will make us wait still longer. Samuel is ordered on his way with a horn of oil to anoint the one whom God has chosen to become king. But Samuel knows nothing more than that whomever YHWH has selected belongs to the family of Jesse in the far southern village of Bethlehem and that YHWH promises to identify him and tell Samuel what to do at the appropriate moment (vv. 1 and 3).

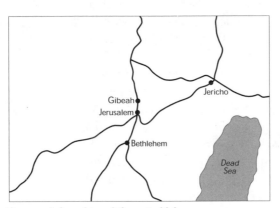

The search for a king shifts to Bethlehem

The search for a king has shifted from Ramah and Gibeah of Benjamin in the north to Judah in the south, and while this is useful geographic information it is also telling symbolic information. Saul's replacement, YHWH's new beginning, is to be found at a distance as far removed from Saul's home as it is expected the new king and his rule will be from Saul's disobedient behavior. Samuel must live with not knowing the details of YHWH's selection process; he must travel in faith, taking God at God's word that, when the time comes, what God wants him to do in that moment will become clear. Not only is Samuel expected to live with and act upon a partial discernment of YHWH's intent, he must do so while overcoming his own fear that "Saul will hear [about the mission] and kill me" (v. 1).

Another lesson for us is woven into the fabric of the story in the narrator's portrayal of YHWH's word to Samuel and the trust it calls for, if Samuel is to leave Ramah for Bethlehem. Partial discernment of God's will in particular situations; personal fear associated with acting as Christ's disciples in threatening circumstances, whether the threat is exclusion of friends, economic costs, or being articulate about our faith; standing with others in an unpopular cause for justice and social change; even facing the anger and alienation of disappointed children—our commitment to follow Christ does not wait until all the facts are in, the costs weighed, and absolute and compelling clarity about what to do emerges. We know the truth, as Samuel does: Doing as God requires in performance of our roles as followers after God's Word can be and often is risky business. But it is the right business for disciples of Christ. Like Samuel, we who are witnesses to God's love at work in our world must quite literally "play it by ear," listening intently through the settings in which we live and serve for God to clarify the choices that are always there and always ours to make. This is not "blind faith" that claims Samuel and us; it is faith that has not seen it all yet and trusts our purposeful God to show us a path of faithful living day by day. Walter Brueggemann puts it this way, speaking of the whole narrative unit that begins with our chapter, "The most interesting interpretive question [arising from the unit] is the way in which the hidden purpose of YHWH is worked out through the awkward and raw events of historical interaction" (Brueggemann, 119).

With the conversation finished between Samuel and YHWH—one that is reminiscent of Moses' protest when sent to pharaoh—the narrative moves rapidly to the events in Bethlehem. What Samuel takes as protection for his journey is YHWH's instruction to tell any who threaten him that he is coming to conduct worship, a role perfectly fea-

> **Who was passed over?**
>
> Jesse had eight sons, only seven of whom are named in the Bible. In birth order, from oldest to youngest, they were: Eliab, Abinadab, Shammah (also called Shimea or Shimei), Nethanel, Raddai, Ozem, and David. (See 1 Chron. 2:13–15.)

sible for Samuel, who seems to have duties as both prophet and priest (see 1 Sam. 13:8–11). In fact, he will offer sacrifice in Bethlehem, and that sacrifice becomes the opportunity for anointing the new king. However short the trip in the narrator's hands, the long process preceding the selection of Saul's successor and the delay in even mentioning the name of David heightens our anticipation of the outcome. One by one, Jesse brings his sons to Samuel; and to Samuel's surprise—and one may imagine Jesse's as well—YHWH does not choose any one of those who, by all appearances, seem "most likely to succeed" (vv. 6–10). In a mild rebuke, YHWH reminds Samuel that, unlike human beings, including ancient and modern readers,

God is not taken by appearance or the standards of attractiveness that typically govern the way human beings see one another. By contrast with superficial features, God sees "into the heart" (v. 7). This teaching is familiar as well from the Second Testament's Gospel of John and the Pauline letters to the Galatians and the Corinthians. In our culture, appearance seems to count above all. Glossy advertisements entice us to believe that dressing one way or another, using particular beauty enhancement products, and having cosmetic surgical procedures can nearly guarantee career success and personal happiness. God, it would seem, has a different way of measuring what counts in the human hope for fulfillment and happiness.

> "So he said to them, 'You are those who justify yourselves in the sight of others; but God knows your hearts; for what is prized by human beings is an abomination in the sight of God.'"—Luke 16:15

But what is it God is looking for in the human heart? The narrator does not tell us exactly, not even when the youngest son of Jesse is brought in from tending sheep and presented to Samuel. Without any explanation from YHWH, Samuel is ordered, "Rise, anoint him, for this is he" (v. 12, author's translation). In Hebrew it takes only four words. Only after he is anointed does the writer reveal the chosen one's name, fulfilling our anticipation: "The Spirit of YHWH came mightily to David from that day forward" (v. 13, author's translation). It is worth noting that the Spirit rushes to David, as it did to those earliest Christians on the Day of Pentecost as a gift (Acts 2); it enters the heart, rather than being something found there already.

Create in Me a Clean Heart, O God

"The Hebrew word for 'heart,' which is here parallel to 'spirit,' does not refer to the seat of the emotions as in English (in Hebrew that would be 'kidneys' or 'bowels'). Rather, 'heart' refers to the mind and the will, that is, the center of the self from which action and loyalty spring."—Bernhard W. Anderson, *Out of the Depths: The Psalms Speak for Us Today*, revised and expanded edition (Philadelphia: Westminster Press, 1983), 97.

Still, though we are not explicitly told what God seeks in the heart of those whom God chooses, implicitly we are invited to remember what we've heard to this point from our Deuteronomic writer. The theme that dominates this history, from its beginning to its end, is the covenant call to the wholehearted love of God, demonstrated in wholehearted obedience to the commandments of God and, negatively, in the watchful avoidance of showing devotion or loyalty to things that are not God. In Hebrew, the "heart" is the seat of human will and decision making, not a fountain of emotions such as we take it to represent. Feelings, of course, are never far from will; obedience requires resolve, for example, and action requires courage. It is this wholeness of human intention, energy, action, and emotion that "heart" represents to the Deuteronomic writer. Remember Samuel's warning to Israel on the verge of making Saul king that failure to keep God's word wholeheartedly would destroy both Israel and her king (chapter 12). What God searches for in the hearts of those, including us, who covenant with God would seem to be this commitment to the wholehearted love of God, love that requires the participation of all that we are—heart, mind, strength, and spirit (see Deut. 6:5 and Mark 12:30).

Is this a counsel of perfection beyond human reach? Is Jeremiah 31 right that the only way humankind can have the kind of heart for which God looks is if God gives it to us, writes God's *Torah* or covenant instruction upon it so that it becomes part of us? That may be the Deuteronomic Historian's conclusion, set so deep within the events of the people of Israel in Jeremiah's prophecies on the edge of the exile. Indeed, one way to look at the redemptive love of God at work in Christ is to see it as an infinite effort to remake our hearts for the love of God and our neighbors, confessing that no one of us is able still to love God wholeheartedly.

Nevertheless, no counsel of perfection nor demand beyond our doing is made in 1 Samuel 16:1–13. What YHWH so sharply demonstrates to Samuel is the difference between human and divine perspectives and the criteria that set them apart. Human beings—even prophets—can be easily misled by what we see or even what we *expect* to see. God, on the other hand, looks into the core of human being, sees into the deepest recesses of our hearts—presumably the good and the bad—and makes judgments and choices accordingly. The lesson from the writer here is not about perfection but perspective, and the encouragement implicitly is that we try to see things from the divine point of view as well and not allow ourselves to be deceived by what does not count in God's economy of love and justice. David is the youngest in the family of Jesse; and he is the one not there. While, as Brueggemann points out, the narrator seems irresistibly drawn to telling us about his appearance, that is not presumably what is attractive to YHWH. The value of the story here is in the surprise and shock that strikes first Samuel and then the readers. Why not one of the other brothers? Why not the first and probably eldest brother with whom Samuel was so taken? Were they bypassed because they lacked something that God did not see in their hearts?

But that is to read too much into the story before us. Two things we know: God makes judgments looking deeply into the human heart, and David is chosen and anointed. Why God chose David and why God did not choose the others we are not told; we only know it had to do with how God saw David "by heart." We could speculate, fairly I think, that whatever God saw in David showed the promise of love for God and willingness to live by the *Torah,* the instruction of God.

> "David is one of the marginal people. He is uncredentialed and has no social claim to make. Those who fastened on to this story most passionately may have been those who, like David, were marginal with no credentials and no social claim. For such people it would be important to assert and celebrate that among the marginal there are beautiful people, that among the little ones there is the potential for greatness. In the hearing of the story are the seeds of hope for all those who joined the company and the narrated imagination of David."—Brueggemann, *First and Second Samuel,* Interpretation, 124.

Suppose we were to take the Deuteronomist's lesson to heart—our hearts. What difference might it make in the way we live, and how could we find the power to change our way of seeing so radically? Is it presumptuous to say we can aim in our life of faith to see things from God's point of view? We are forced to admit from the outset the danger that lurks here. We may fall into thinking that while trying to see as God sees— that is, from the inside out rather than the outside in—the world around us, our neighbors, and, importantly, ourselves, we may deceive ourselves into thinking we are god-like, thereby making idols of ourselves. What may save us from such self-delusion and arrogance is the confession that we are not God. We are human beings, called by God, graced by God with love, and looking for ways to return the favor to God and to others. In the end, we are and must be human beings trying in faith and by faith to look at life as we live it with God's eyes of discerning love, knowing we cannot see with complete clarity. For now, we can see only as if looking into a cloudy surface, as if looking in a slightly distorting mirror, to use Paul's lovely image (1 Cor. 13:12). Our heartfelt intention is not to claim God's power of perception but to name God's way of seeing, contrasted with ordinary human practice, in a way that calls us to a *more faithful practice of discipleship discernment.* The phrase I used above seems to me suggestive of that aim: *to see the world we live in daily from the inside out, rather than the outside in.* This, I suggest, is the logic of seeing through the eyes of faith and a logic that participates in the divine point of view.

Christians practicing faith by this logic of "heart-seeing" are looking at others and at life through a storied perspective that pays special attention to the heart of God made flesh in Jesus Christ. Such "heart-seeing," conversely, pays less attention to wondering about the character and behavior of others in the human community and the created order, to whom we are sent as Christ's disciples. It works this way: We know, in Christ, God loves generously, without boundaries of race, gender, economic status, educational, business, or political achievement. Yet these are the kinds of boundaries that separate us from one another and often from ourselves, and restrict love to those whom we like or who are like us, reserving hate for everyone and everything on the other side of the lines. The inside-out logic of "heart-seeing" requires disciples to follow the Teacher, and love without boundaries, reserving hate for only the destructive, demonic forces that turn human hearts into seedbeds of misery, pain, unhappiness, meaninglessness, spite, prejudice, infidelity, or greed. Generous love, we are taught by our radical Teacher, can overcome these destructive powers. It can do so because it lures from the human heart what God must also see there: human potential and possibility for re-creation and new creation. Similarly, God's heart-felt compassion for poor, oppressed, and excluded people, and for people enslaved to economic structures, the quest for power and prestige, or false promises of success and security through the accumulation of wealth, calls for disciple discernment and response. Heart-seeing people of faith are encouraged to rethink their own lives—that is, search their own hearts for what matters from God's point of view. Having looked into ourselves, we are prepared for God's invitation to join God in working for the justice of love, letting go the bonds of contemporary versions of slavery to open a way to God's promise of a full and abundant life in the love of Christ.

The closing comment about David in 1 Samuel 16:1–13 brings us to a close here. How may we be enabled or empowered to see in this new way of faith, from the inside out, rather than the outside in? Upon his anointing, the Spirit of YHWH came mightily to David from that day forward. Thus God equipped the one chosen for the service upon which

---

📖 Want to Know More?

About providence? See Shirley C. Guthrie, *Christian Doctrine*, rev. ed. (Louisville, Ky.: Westminster John Knox Press, 1994), 166–91; Daniel L. Migliore, *The Power of God* (Philadelphia: Westminster Press, 1983), 80–90.

About anointing? See Leland Ryken, James C. Wilhoit, and Tremper Longman III, eds., *Dictionary of Biblical Imagery* (Downers Grove, Ill.: InterVarsity Press, 1998), 33–34.

About the sacrifice of animals? See Werner H. Schmidt, *The Faith of the Old Testament: A History* (Philadelphia: Westminster Press, 1983), 127–32.

anointing sent him. I called attention earlier to the parallel between this proclamation about David and Luke's declaration about the experience of the followers of Jesus, upon whom the Spirit rushed mightily on the Day of Pentecost. We may take our comfort and our energy from both these visions. The anointing that signals our belonging to God takes place with the water of baptism. By God's grace and love, we are accompanied by the Holy Spirit from that time forward. We are enabled to see inside out, as I've been calling the way of discernment that joins us to God's perspective. Paul's way of describing life in Christ, in fact, is "life in the Spirit" or "walking in the Spirit." This life he contrasts with life before baptism into the body of Christ and the gift of the Spirit of Christ. The former life he calls "life in the flesh," which can only see the world as it was before Christ came. This kind of seeing "in the flesh" I have been calling "seeing from the outside in," because it is bound to all the frantic efforts of self-achievement and self-satisfaction that characterize taking life "just the way it is." Those in Christ, who walk in the Spirit, Paul believes, know the truth about "things as they really are." And the truth is they are not as they appear to be; in Christ reality has changed completely, and those in Christ must walk in the vision of the new creation, not the old one. Sin remains, we know, at work in us. St. Paul's sorrow is ours: The good we want to do we do not do, and the evil we do not want, we do (see Rom. 7:21–25).

Wonderfully, however, eagerness to forgive, heal, and restore relationships remains close to God's heart. The sacramental moment in which we may celebrate God's promise of our renewal is the Lord's Supper. There we taste the death and life of Christ and may find our eyes opened to the heart of God. There we share a vision of the new creation, the world not simply as it will be but as it truly is even now. It is a meal nurturing a new way of seeing and being alive in Christ.

? Questions for Reflection

1. God chastises Samuel, saying that while humans may judge each other based on outward appearance, God "looks on the heart." Can you say the same about yourself?
2. What must Samuel have been thinking as he watched God pass over the first seven sons of Jesse? What do you think Jesse was thinking?

3. Discuss the concept of "heart-seeing" as defined in this session. Is it asking too much to hope that more human beings practice "heart-seeing"? Do you think *you* can?
4. Read 1 Samuel 16:13 and compare it to Acts 2:2–4. How are these passages similar? How are they different?

6

2 Samuel 7:1–17

A Promise of Steadfast Love Forever

Let's start this time with some big observations before we look more closely at this remarkable passage. First, we have taken a large leap from the last text, 1 Samuel 16, which told of David's anointing as king, to a chapter in 2 Samuel which portrays David firmly in power in a new royal city, Jerusalem. The struggle between David and Saul, as Saul tried desperately to hold onto royal power, has occupied the narrative over which we have passed. In the end, clearly in this passage, David has completely replaced Saul. The word of God to Samuel in chapter 16 has been fulfilled.

Next, in the larger context of the Deuteronomic writer's history of Israel, 2 Samuel 7 is regarded by scholars as close to the heart and soul of the whole story of the monarchy. Speaking of its significance, Walter Brueggemann writes, "[This passage] occupies the dramatic and theological center of the entire Samuel corpus. Indeed, this is one of the most crucial texts in the Old Testament for evangelical faith" (Brueggemann, 253). With his latter comment, Brueggemann extends the significance of 2 Samuel 7 well beyond the Deuteronomic History, underscoring its place as a text important to the gospel and to the practice of Christian faith. I will come back to this claim in a bit, but first let us return to consider the place of 2 Samuel 7 in the Deuteronomic writer's history of Israel. This is important to us because it provides clues to how this passage has been and may be a bearer of meaning regarding Israel's identity and our own.

The Deuteronomic writer appears to have composed his history by structuring Israel's past into three periods: the exodus and conquest (roughly Deuteronomy and Joshua), the time of the judges

(Judges and 1 Samuel), and the period of the monarchy (2 Samuel and 1 and 2 Kings). The rise of the monarchy and its establishment under David clearly stand, by this scheme, at the apex of the entire history. Second Samuel 7, with its affirmations of David's firm hold on leadership, his rest from enemies, the security of Israel's place in the land, and a dynasty that will last forever, is an ending point for the struggles of conquest, the insecurities of judgeship, and the initial crisis of monarchy. At the same time, this chapter provides the bell-weather for the kings who will follow David: They will be judged by their proximity to the model of "my servant David." Significantly, this phrase parallels the writer's designation of Moses as "my servant Moses." As Moses dominates the first half of the Deuteronomic History, David is the symbol of the just and righteous king that pervades the age of the monarchy, becoming the standard against which all future rulers will be measured.

Remembering that the Deuteronomic History most likely was written during the time of Israel's exile, the time of David, so full of promise and hope, has become something of a "golden age." The writer's message inlaid in the history he has written calls for Israel in exile to look again at the beginning in promise with David. It urges recall of the extraordinary promise of God to David's heirs to love them as a parent loves a child. It begs exiled Israel to remember and admit the sins of David's successors and their own complicity in them, and return now to YHWH with hope born of the extravagance of God's love. Hope still abides for a restored political Israel under Davidic rule at the time the Deuteronomic writer's work is presented. After the exile, that hope will give way to political reality and a history of sad subjugation under foreign powers. And groups in the postexilic community itself dispute the wisdom of any further effort to revive the institution of monarchy. But that is beyond the time of our writer.

As hope for a restored Israel under a Davidic king fades, the ideal is projected into a hoped-for future in the shape of *messianism,* the expectation of a Messiah who will come at a time of divine transformation, when the kingdoms of this earth will become the kingdom of God. Brueggemann writes, "Out of this oracle [in chapter 7] there emerges the hope held by Israel in every season that there is a coming David who will right wrong and establish good governance. That one may be hidden in the vagaries of history, may experience resistance from the recalcitrance of injustice and unrighteousness, but nevertheless there is one coming who will make things right" (Brueggemann, 257). I would add here a caution. In Israel's history of ideas, the hope for a coming messiah takes many forms. While at the heart of any is the recollection of David's favor with God and God's generous promises to David's heirs, we would be mistaken to speak of messianic hope as a unified concept in Israel or in Judaism. For example, I have heard countless sermons that contrast Jesus Messiah's behavior—healing, suffering, and dying—with Jewish expectations of *the* Messiah as a conquering warrior, overthrowing the hated Romans. Even John the Baptist, first so sure of Jesus' power to "winnow" the wheat from the chaff in devastating judgment, sends his disciples later to inquire, "Are you he or shall we look for another?" (Matt. 3:11–12 and 11:3). The significance of Jesus' response to John that focuses on the healing work of Jesus Messiah (11:5) is not found by contrasting it with a supposed fixed Jewish expectation. Judaism's understanding of messiah was more fluid than that in Jesus' day. And the concept of messiah has remained too rich to be constrained into one voice. That is important to Christians as we look at our own affirmations about Jesus Messiah against this multicolored background in Judaism.

Which brings us to the third big thing we need to consider about 2 Samuel 7:1–17. It is hard for us as Christian readers to finish reading these verses, with their culminating promise to David, "I will surely establish your rule forever in my presence; your throne will be secure forever" (v. 16, author's translation), and not immediately think of Jesus Christ. Again Brueggemann comments, "It goes without saying that this text does not intend to point to Jesus. At the same time, however, we may see how easy and natural it was for the community around Jesus to seize upon this text as a way to understand the reality of Jesus" (Brueggemann, 257–58). If we are to hear what God may be saying to us through 2 Samuel 7, we must make the very difficult move of setting aside initially any impulse we may have to overlook the voice of this passage in favor of rushing to our Christian beliefs concerning Jesus' messiahship.

It is important for us as we listen to 2 Samuel 7 to remember that the church turned to this passage for help in articulating what the early Christians believed about Jesus and God's work through him. The writer of Luke's Gospel especially has drawn on passages, phrases, and images from the books of Samuel to portray Jesus. Examples might include the close relationship between the "Magnificat" and Mary's Song (Luke 1:46–55) and the Song of Hannah (1 Samuel 2). We can look at old Simeon, the righteous one in Israel, celebrating the birth of Jesus Messiah before Mary in the Temple (Luke 2:25–35), and be reminded of Eli, Hannah, and the child Samuel in the sanctuary in 1 Samuel 1. Finally, Luke describes Jesus as increasing "in wisdom and in years, and in divine and human favor" (Luke 2:52) in language reminiscent of 1 Samuel 2:26. This use of the First Testament scripture to explain for early Christians who Jesus is and how Jesus is related to the hopes of faith in the communities from which the first Christian writing arose is important for us to recognize.

For us, however, things have changed. We embrace both Testaments as the Word of God, so there is more to "scripture" for us than what the early Christian communities and the Gospel writers or Paul meant by "scripture." In addition, we generally use very different methods for interpreting scripture than those common to the Christian writers. This includes, among other things, not using scripture for polemical purposes like those that preoccupied early Christians trying to establish legitimacy for their beliefs in their society. Finally, like the early Christians, we do search the scriptures for insight and guidance for responding to questions of faith and the practice of faith arising from our life together in congregations living within our own largely secular cultures. However, our questions are necessarily different and the actions we may take in response are likely to be quite different, too. Jesus' world and that of Christians immediately after him was largely a sacred one, not a secular one like ours. All this means we are called to let the light of passages from both Testaments illuminate our practice of faith in Christ, without the kind of polemical selectivity of texts that was so necessary to the earliest Christians' search for their own identity. Concern for our identity remains critical, but times, questions, and ways of reading and interpreting scripture have changed.

Let's turn now to look at the passage before us. 2 Samuel 7 divides readily into two parts. The first, verses 1–17, contains an oracle from God that Nathan, the prophet, is directed to deliver to David, the king. The second part, verses 18–29, is a prayer offered by David in grateful response to the words of God that Nathan has delivered. We are focusing on the first part and, in it, Nathan's oracle in verses 4–16. The opening three verses set the context for the prophetic vision, and the last verse testifies to Nathan's faithful delivery of the words of

YHWH to King David. In the most succinct fashion, the narrator describes the historic moment of the chapter. In verse 1 we are told, in a long clause that is not even a sentence, that once David was settled in his royal house (palace), he decided it was the right moment to build a house (temple) as a permanent dwelling place for the Ark of the Covenant. Nathan, in language that draws us back to the Spirit coming mightily upon David in 1 Samuel 16, gives the idea his blessing. When night comes and the prophet sleeps, however, a divine oracle comes to him contradicting his encouragement to David.

The oracle is bound to the introduction with a play on the word "house": David wants to build a house for the Ark—a temple, in other words, for YHWH. But YHWH has another kind of "house" in mind for David and promises him a dynasty, a "house forever." Hebrew allows for this remarkable use of *bayit*, which can mean "house," "household," "palace," "temple," or "lineage, dynasty" in such a variegated way.

> "This passage consists of a divine oracle (vv. 1–17) and a responding prayer (vv. 18–29). It occupies the dramatic and theological center of the entire Samuel corpus. Indeed, this is one of the most crucial texts in the Old Testament for evangelical faith."—Brueggemann, *First and Second Samuel*, Interpretation, 253.

Our writer takes full advantage of the variety of meanings available, creating something both significant in meaning and delightful to read. David, his own house built, thanks to God's presence with him through all the trials that have led to peace at last in Jerusalem, has great plans to create a Holy Place in the City of David in which YHWH may be enthroned. While perhaps not without political motivations, since royal cities in the ancient world invariably included a temple or shrine for the protecting deity, on another level David's intention is presented by the narrator as an act of faith. David and the people are at last secure, no longer living in tents or hiding out in caves but now living in a palace in a fortified city. Should not the Ark of God, symbolizing the Holy One who made it all possible, also have a dwelling place that is not temporary and transitory?

There is something of the same impulse, perhaps, in our own sense of urgency when a new congregation is founded to build a sanctuary, to establish a "permanent residence," as it were, for the church. Anyone who has been part of a new church development knows how setting up chairs in the local school or some other rented space for Sunday worship, only to have to take them down and store them until next week, can quickly grow old. Identity seems to urge upon us a place to be, and our houses and our houses of worship provide a crucial sense of "where" that helps us define "who" we are. Sometimes we have feared that place might overwhelm purpose, that as a congregation we may be suffering from an "edifice" complex that has confused our identity. On such occasions we have longed for or experimented with "churches without walls." But for most of us a place is needed, a church home that combines the sense of "home" remarkable in family and the sense of "home" that speaks of residence or place. The danger, of course, lies in the possibility of the church home or sanctuary becoming an *object* of worship rather than a *place* of worship, as if God were somehow captive to the places we build in God's name.

The Ark of the Covenant

God's rhetorical response to David's nascent plans (vv. 4–7) is sometimes seen as a rebuke of David. In this view, David's plan is seen as a threat to the freedom of God and an effort to control the presence of God. However, as I have suggested already by illustration, another possible interpretation sees the issue not as the freedom of God but the well-being of the community of faith.

Again, we may appeal to our own experience: In making plans to build or reconstruct our houses of worship, it may be hoped that, as this passage suggests, whether to do so is related directly to discerning God's mission for a community of faith. Perhaps it is to build; perhaps it is to wait to build until the time is right from God's point of view, insofar as wisdom is given us to see it. The relationship between God and the places we build for worship is an issue of faith worth probing thoughtfully, and you may wish to undertake such discussion as you consider this passage. What rings throughout these 17 verses is the priority God gives to acting graciously toward David, his heirs, and, through them, to Israel into the future. And what seems appropriate in response are acts on our part that are similarly gracious and open-handed that "build up" others, imagery that the Ephesians letter uses in the Second Testament to describe the work of mature believers. Building a building is not enough; God requires that priority be given to building justice and love and constructing ways of healing and hope for all. Then the building, whether sanctuary, fellowship hall, or education space, becomes a place of purpose and celebration to the glory of God.

My wife and I have a friend whose constant generosity toward us, as well as others, leaves us routinely shaking our heads in amazement. She is a person whose openhearted spirit is a loud and public testimony to her faith in Christ. Yet it is offered with an unassuming, almost natural quality that belies the consciousness I know she brings to her many thoughtful acts and gestures. She is, for me, a living reminder of the generosity of God. Over the years, my wife and I have been fortunate to have many friends for whom the adjective "gracious" would be apt. But what makes this particular friend of ours unique in this vein is her uncanny ability to see below the surface of an opportunity to be thoughtful or kind and then fill that moment to overflowing in unimagined and unexpected ways that nurture and nourish those around her. That kind of seeing is remarkable to me; indeed, I would call it a gift of God.

I tell you about my friend—and you no doubt know people just like her—because it may be a way to understand the kind of generosity and overabundance of grace that YHWH displays toward David in 2 Samuel 7:1–17. It is, of course, a fact of our faith that we see God's continuing creative and redemptive work in the world through the lives and agency of humankind. The incarnation of God, so fully visible in Christ, continues in an array of more modest manifestations in our lives and in our relations with others and with the environment in which we participate. God's generosity and over fulfillment of God's promises worked out in human history is a powerful theme ringing through what otherwise might appear to be a remote story about a divine surprise for an Israelite king in the 10th century B.C.E.

Consider particularly verses 8–16. In Nathan's vision, YHWH sends the prophet to David with a divine word that reminds David of what God has already done for him and promises still more blessing in the future, indeed, as far into the future as imaginable. David has done nothing to earn his way to this place of power and time of peace and rest. All this has come to pass because "I took you from following sheep to become a prince over all my people Israel, and I have been with you everywhere you have traveled, and I struck down all your enemies" (vv. 8–9, author's translation). These words recall the passage we studied in 1 Samuel 16, when Samuel and the Spirit of God anointed the young shepherd David and the Spirit of God came mightily upon David, as the narrator put it, "from that time forward." The Spirit of God has empowered David to this position, enabling him to overcome serious and dangerous opposition to establishing his legitimacy as Israel's king; he has not earned what he now enjoys.

Still, God is not finished showing kindness to David; Nathan's oracle offers an even brighter future for David and Israel. YHWH promises David a "great name" or reputation, as others in the land enjoy. The reference here is blurry; it likely refers to a place of prominence among the leaders of neighboring nation-states. But on another level it seems also to reflect the "great name" David is to have in the memory of the Israelites, a reputation as a righteous and just king with whom the Spirit of God dwelt constantly.

Want to Know More?

About the exile? See Celia Brewer Marshall, *A Guide through the Old Testament* (Louisville, Ky.: Westminster John Knox Press, 1989), 114.

About messianism? See Celia Brewer Marshall, *A Guide through the New Testament* (Louisville, Ky.: Westminster John Knox Press, 1994), 33.

David's name is joined in Israel's history with that of Moses, Abraham, Sarah, Deborah, and, in the Second Testament, Jesus. And there is more: YHWH promises David security and peace from his enemies and a place of peace in which Israel may dwell (v. 10). Finally comes the most extravagant, surprising, and intimate gift from God (vv. 12–16). David's kingship shall not be buried with him. Rather, God promises to establish a "house" to follow after him, so that the rule he has established will continue forever. Here we need to keep in mind what we know of David. The Spirit of God abides with him in all that he does, so the promise of an everlasting throne is, at the same time, a promise that the Spirit of God will continue to dwell with David's successors. This is a note that is both comforting and, in some situations, *dis*comforting.

The image the divine oracle includes to underscore this "relationship forever" with YHWH is telling. God promises to be as a parent to a child to the successors of David. The metaphor suggests a relationship of unconditional love; that is, love that is unearned and generously given simply because of the relationship. I count, for example, among the most precious days in my life the ones I spent with my wife sharing in the birth of our children. The rush of love I experienced the moment each was pushed into the world was incomparable. That, I think, is the kind of love God experiences, in our passage, at the birth of David's house. Parental love, however, includes responsibility for discipline and correction, too. And the oracle acknowledges this by promising that, when David's heirs sin—as no doubt they will—they will be chastised or punished, but God's "steadfast love" (v. 15) will not be taken away.

Clearly there is much of importance for us in these verses recalling God's extravagant love toward David and David's house. The promises extend through faith to us. We are recipients of God's grace and unconditional love through our life together in Christ. What Nathan saw as a vision for David's future in God's love, we see in the image of God as love in Christ. We need not say, however, that God's unconditional love is experienced *only* in Christ, and 2 Samuel 7 cautions us against any exclusivism that restrains God's love. It is gospel enough for us to witness to the love of God we see and know through our own experience living in Christ and walking in the Spirit of Christ day by day. For us, in Christ, God's promised "relationship forever" presses us toward the future in hope, locating our meaning and purpose in life in the context of loving God as children beloved by God. It also invites us to believe in a life forever with God, an everlasting life by contrast with David's everlasting throne. Christ's resurrection bids us to think so boldly of God's generous, steadfast, and neverending love toward us.

A closing and perhaps ironic word about the conditions of unconditional love. Many of us have in our soul an impulse that finds it next to impossible to live with grace—unmerited gifts of love from God. Proclamation of such everlasting, unearned generosity, though it may be the heart of the Christian gospel, is tough to make and tough to swallow in our world of cause and effect where, as my father used to say, the common wisdom is "There is no such thing as a free lunch." This word of God's unconditional love for us, which in Christ is an "us" that includes all humanity, always brings worries to the surface. The usual question arising is something like, "Why should anyone act ethically or obey God's will if there is no judgment

> "Cheap grace is the grace we bestow on ourselves. Cheap grace is the preaching of forgiveness without requiring repentance, baptism without church discipline, Communion without confession, absolution without personal confession. Cheap grace is grace without discipleship, grace without the cross, grace without Jesus Christ, living and incarnate. . . . Costly grace is the gospel which must be *sought* again and again, the gift which must be *asked* for, the door at which a man must *knock*. Such grace is *costly* because it calls us to follow, and it is *grace* because it calls us to follow *Jesus Christ*. . . . Above all, it is *costly* because it cost God the life of his Son. . . . Above all, it is *grace* because God did not reckon his Son too dear a price to pay for our life, but delivered him up for us. Costly grace is the Incarnation of God."—Dietrich Bonhoeffer, *The Cost of Discipleship* (New York: Macmillan Co., 1960), 36–37.

on and no consequence for our actions?" The question, of course, reflects an age-old struggle in the church between "justification by faith" and "justification by works." Second Samuel 7, therefore, can teach us something about what theologian and martyr Dietrich Bonhoeffer called "costly grace," as opposed to "cheap grace." Unconditional love does not nullify standards of behavior within the love relationship. We do not love, in this case, to earn love; we love because we are already loved. Love in Christ, so generous and life-giving, requires living in the Spirit of Christ by what one might call an "ethics of the Spirit." This ethic, which in an earlier lesson I called "seeing from the inside out," looks for opportunities to express in daily interaction the kind of freeing, healing, re-creating experience for others that we know by the steadfast grace of God in Christ. You may want to sharpen the meaning of an "ethics of the Spirit" in your own context and in light of your vision of life in the Spirit of Christ. The chastisement that comes to us when we fail to live in Christ is, as Nathan's vision describes it, a loss in our relationship with others, and a sense of being at the mercy of the winds that swirl around us. The wonderful news is, thank God, we need not fear the loss of God's claim of love upon us.

 ## Questions for Reflection

1. Why was YHWH resistant to the idea of David's building a permanent resting place for the Ark?
2. Has your congregation ever succumbed to the temptation of making the church an object of worship rather than a place of worship?
3. In Unit 4 we saw God punish Saul for what may seem to us to be a minor transgression. 1 Samuel 16:14 even tells us that "the spirit of the Lord departed from Saul." Yet here God promises unconditional love to David "forever," saying that God will not take his steadfast love from David even "when he commits iniquity." How do you rationalize these two actions of God?
4. Read the definitions of costly grace and cheap grace. Have you ever practiced cheap grace? Do you think it is easy, or even possible, for people today to practice costly grace?

7

2 Samuel 11:1–27

David and Bathsheba

If one were asked to complete the phrase "David and . . . ," my hunch is that two names would compete for the most likely choice: Goliath and Bathsheba. These two names are associated with stories from the Bible that are known to children and adults from church folks to the general population. Big money movies, cartoons, television mini-series, books, and plays have all provided visual images that claim to "bring the story alive" and spread the stories among millions of people. (My view, which you could guess by now, is that the literature of 1 and 2 Samuel is quite powerful and lively enough to challenge and hold our attention and imagination, and need not rely on Hollywood or New York to "bring it to life.") The story of David's heroic battle with Goliath (1 Samuel 17), with its classic portrayal of a young, ill-equipped person fighting for a righteous cause against a monstrous and wicked enemy, has entered our speech as symbolic imagery for characterization of battles in life against overwhelming odds. It is a story to encourage, to bolster the faith and confidence of those under siege from forces that seem irresistible, where failure is certain. Perhaps that is why we especially provide children with access to the story, as Sunday school literature of all sorts readily demonstrates. Perhaps that is why "Davy and Goliath," aimed at the moral development of young viewers, was such a popular cartoon during its run on television in the 1960s and 1970s.

"David and Bathsheba," however, is a story for a time and a place out of earshot (and sight) of young children. It would fit the "after family hour" viewing time slots beautifully. In fact, a made-for-TV movie that took up the story aired at 9 P.M. with the equivalent of a PG rating for "violence and adult situations." If the story receives serious attention at all in church education it is typically in adult classes. Some may venture its use with adolescents. But that seems very risky to many, given the touchy nature of teaching youth through material that is clearly sexual in nature and innuendo and raises serious questions about appropriate moral behavior between men and women in a context of Christian faith. Frankly, I think many of us want the church to raise just such important moral questions with our youth. But, as teachers and youth leaders, the strong American attitude that moral teaching belongs in the home and is the inviolable right of parents hangs heavy over the possibility of doing so in classes or meetings. So adult Sunday school seems to be the preferred venue.

"David and Goliath" provides lessons in courage in the face of terrible threat, reliance on relationship with God, trust in God's purpose, and self-sacrifice for the sake of others in desperate need. By contrast, "David and Bathsheba" presents the other side of David's character, purposefully hidden from public view, including ours, until now. Nothing we know about David through the narratives studied so far has prepared us for the disturbing and painful look into his heart and mind that we get in 2 Samuel 11. That adds to the shock value of the story. It causes within its readers and hearers what educators and others who study how we think and learn call "dissonance." Dissonance results when we experience a sudden challenge to the way we have typically thought or felt about something; it results from seeing or hearing about someone acting or speaking in ways incongruent with what we have come to expect of them. An expression of shock like, "I don't believe it! They would never do such a thing!" conveys the feeling. Dissonance explains part of why we feel so shocked and find so unbelievable the terrible occasions of shootings and violence in our public schools. Schools, as one mother on such a tragic occasion put it, are supposed to be safe places. Dissonance describes the gap between the reality of violence in schools and the expectation that they should be what they have always appeared to be: namely, safe and nonviolent environments in which children may learn. The positive value potential in experiences of dissonance is the need they present to rethink how and what we've held to be true and to learn to think in a different way about what has been so familiar. To continue with the school violence illustration, for Christians, tragedies like these may create dissonance concerning the way we have thought about God's relationship to us and human affairs more generally. The impulse for vengeance against perpetrators in these instances, for example, may challenge what we hold to be true about forgiveness and unconditional love of neighbor, requiring us to do a good deal of soul-searching to come to a place where we can say afresh what we truly believe.

> "We are not prepared for such a David. What began as a lustful whim developed into an enormous sex-and-murder crime. How does such sin happen? As with most sins, gradually and unobtrusively."— Peterson, *First and Second Samuel*, Westminster Bible Companion, 182.

Dissonance, then, may be a way of thinking about what our writer is doing with the presentation of David in the story of his abuse and rape of Bathsheba, his efforts at a royal "cover-up," and the murder of her husband, Uriah the Hittite, along with an untold number of Uriah's military comrades. And if we have uncovered a clue to our writer's intention, perhaps we can also open ourselves to the challenges that the experience of a "different David" may make upon our ways of thinking and being with others and with God. For, as we could have guessed, this story of David, Bathsheba, Uriah, and YHWH is as much about us as it is about them. How that is so remains to be seen. We will discover how this story can confront us in our day and age, however, only by letting ourselves be drawn into it. We need to see its truth from the inside as the participants in a human drama about all-too-familiar human behavior: lust, greed, abuse of trust and power, self-indulgence, hiding from truth, and the murder of innocents.

Our writer has not taken us into the dark alleys and poor neighborhoods of the city to meet such human characteristics. Nor are we led to hideouts of robbers or the underworld of organized crime. We are invited into the king's house—the best house in the best neighborhood in the best city. We are in the best of company, the model home of the model citizen and the most righteous person we know. That's what brings the story so close to home for all of us. Not that we live in palaces, though our homes may seem so to the poor and homeless in our communities. But, like David, many of us enjoy social and financial privilege, solid status as citizens in our communities, and good educational and job opportunities that offer possibilities of life being relatively comfortable and secure. In David, we see a person who has been the beneficiary of countless blessings, as 2 Samuel 7 made so abundantly clear to us; a person of privilege and standing to whom the welfare of all Israel and Judah has been entrusted; a person to look up to. Opportunities for living a good life, alas, hold simultaneously occasions for destructive behavior. That is a truth we know, but it is one easily forgotten—until something like this story of David demands we remember and give account of ourselves.

Professor Brueggemann helpfully summarizes the scholarly debate regarding the larger unit of narrative to which chapter 11 belongs, as well as chapters 12 and 18, at which we will look in the two sessions to follow (Brueggemann, 265–66). What is contested is the identity of the writer, the date of composition and, to some extent, the exact beginning and ending points to the narrative unit. All agree, however, that at least chapters 9–20 are so similar in style and content that they belong together. There is also agreement that the style that hallmarks this writing, with its intimate and emotional look into the house of David, differs from that of the earlier chapters we have seen. Not only is writing from an "insider's" view remarkable in this author's work, but the depth of human analysis artistically conveyed is profound. It is this artistic gift that invites readers, like ourselves, into the story and, consequently, into our own hearts and minds.

As Brueggemann wisely implies, we need not solve all the mysteries of literary composition or dating to draw upon this story of David and his family for the wisdom it may offer us for living in our time as people of Christian faith. We can say that this unit of chapters 9–20, whatever its origin, has now been joined intentionally to the narratives we have studied. That means we may fairly look for connections between what we are reading and what we have read. In the case of 2 Samuel 11:1–27, to be specific, we approach our task of careful listening with the wonderful news of 2 Samuel 7:1–17 still ringing in our ears. YHWH's promise to David was to build his house, to establish him among the great figures of history, to give him rest from his enemies and the nation a place of rest and peace. Above all, YHWH promised to David's house an everlasting relationship like that of a parent to a child; a relationship of accountability to *Torah*, the law of Moses; and chastisement on occasions of failure to heed God's word. But YHWH also promised continuous and unbroken *hesed* —"steadfast love" forever. In the chapters between 7 and 11, David has offered an eloquent prayer of thanksgiving for God's gracious promises and proven himself victorious in battle and magnanimous toward the one remaining member of Saul's house. So far he has acted with the same nobility and righteousness we have come to expect. Chapter 11, however, presents a new and different kind of challenge to David's character. It gives us the first opportunity to see how one with whom God has dealt so graciously will respond when the doors are shut to the public, the press corps has gone, and the boots of the battlefield have given way to carpet slippers.

I do not wish to retell the story with you this time. The narrative's subtle and dramatic quality works effectively on our imaginations without the paraphrase of an interpreter. Once read and slowly savored, however, features of the story emerge that are potentially important in guiding our search for its meaning for us. These are the moments, actions, thoughts, or words that push themselves hard into our consciousness. As we read and listen, we wonder:

- How could that happen?

- What does that word or phrase mean or imply, since it is not a familiar expression?

- What are the "operative social norms" in an ancient monarchical context like this one bound by a Mosaic covenantal morality?

- How do they differ from ours, and does their difference contribute to our shock or other response to what we hear in the story?

Questions like these that arise spontaneously from our thoughts and feelings begin building a bridge between our world and the world of the text that will prove strong enough to bear the weight of meaning for our lives. Striking in our story are the sharp contrasts in settings, personal status, and individual character throughout. For example:

- David stays at home, for the first time, while Joab and the army fight in the fields, besieging an Ammonite city. As Brueggemann notes, David acts like a royal commander-in-chief, depending on military intelligence reports and on the skill of his field general, Joab (Brueggemann, 273).

- David enjoys the peace and luxury of his palace in Jerusalem, while his former military comrades live under the strict discipline of battle and field rations. Could it be that his new role grows quickly boring to a man accustomed to being in the thick of the fray? Spare time and opportunity for self-indulgence are natural to the style of life David is enjoying.

- David is king, with great royal power and privilege and equally great temptation to abuse them, to use them to "take," rather than "give," as Samuel warned at the inception of the monarchy in Israel (1 Samuel 8; see also Unit 2). Bathsheba is someone unknown to David, a woman without a name until he wants to make use of her; and a woman without a name when he is finished (see 11:3–5).

- David enjoys the royal privilege of many wives, unfortunate signs of his victories and alliances, taken for purposes that serve the state. They, too, with occasional exception, are nameless; more properly than persons in the royal state of affairs. Bathsheba, on the other hand, is another man's wife—Uriah, the Hittite, a sojourner in Israel in the service of the king in Joab's army in the field. Sojourners, you will recall, as earlier audiences surely did, are non-Israelites under special protection in the Mosaic moral code, entitled to special care and generosity on the part of the covenant people (see Ex. 22:20; Deut. 10:19).

- David's behavior reflects a willingness to use his power for self-gratification. The one most dedicated to abiding by the Word of God, from whom service to God's people and trustworthiness and honesty are most expected, casts all trust aside to serve his own pleasure and cover up the consequences of his lustful appetite.

- Uriah, on the other hand, though a foreigner and mercenary to Israel's cause, keeps the trust placed in him, proves himself loyal to his commander, the king, and to his comrades, who live sparsely on the field of battle and are bound to a vow of sexual abstinence while at war.

No love, care, or compassion toward Bathsheba is present; only lust, greed, violation, and abuse of power.

- We are told nothing about Uriah's relationship to Bathsheba, suggesting that it is not an important issue in the story in the writer's mind. Silence allows us to assume, given Uriah's known character, that he honored her in a fashion appropriate to the ethos of the culture in which they were living. David, by contrast, abused her, first by taking her from her husband's home, thereby committing adultery, and, secondly by treating her as an object for his lustful satisfaction. The narrative is cold in its description of David's rape of Bathsheba. As a woman subject of the king, she cannot be said to have been a "consenting adult," which makes David's crime against her, by our standards, more despicable than "adultery," though it is still that. No love, care, or compassion toward Bathsheba is present; only lust, greed, violation, and abuse of power.

• Finally, two comments artfully connect David's last word and YHWH's first word in the narrative. While evident in Hebrew, the writer's art here is hard to see in English translation. To the messenger who brings the news of Uriah's death, along with many others lost in a "suicide mission" against the enemy's walls, David says, "Tell Joab, 'Do not let this matter trouble (*yera‘*) you . . .'" (v. 25). We might say, "Do not take it personally; let it go; don't brood on it." YHWH has been a silent bystander until now. But now the narrator describes YHWH's feelings with a final word that leaves no doubt that nothing that has happened has gone unnoticed by God: "What David did was evil (*yera‘*) in YHWH's eyes" (v. 27). YHWH takes it all very personally.

Anyone who has lived through the last three decades of the 20th century cannot help but see at least two well-publicized incidents in our mind's eye as we read this account of David's palace behavior. Again, recalling them and the feelings and questions they raised in and among us helps us move from David's palace to our own public square and private lives. A caution here may be helpful. Inviting reflection and conversation about these two highly charged events that swept over the United States and the world *can become* a "rabbit track" away from David and Bathsheba. Rather than illuminating feelings, attitudes, and perspectives we have experienced that draw us closer to understanding 2 Samuel 11:1–27, we risk being drawn away into easier debate over events closer to us.

What's a Sojourner?

A sojourner was one who was not of Israelite descent but who lived with the Hebrews. Thus, as a sojourner, Uriah was "not a full citizen, yet he had recognized rights and duties. . . . He was under the protection of God, and the Israelites were charged to treat him kindly."— *The New Westminster Dictionary of the Bible*, 910.

Two events flooded my mind while reading this story. First came the recent impeachment of President Clinton, resulting from his abuse of power by sexual engagement with a former White House intern. Second was President Richard Nixon's attempted cover-up in the Watergate break-in, which led to articles of impeachment being approved and, ultimately, the President's resignation in 1974. In both cases, I think, we were horrified yet at the same time fascinated as these tragic dramas played out on a *very public* stage, given the television coverage provided. Both cases involved evil perpetrated by leaders from whom good and responsible behavior was rightly expected. Both cases involved behavior so repugnant to the public moral code that the credibility that leadership requires seemed terminally wounded. In both cases we saw people very much like ourselves, though in high office, caught in webs of self-destruction wound from fibers of lust, greed, jealousy, anger, lies, betrayal, and disregard for others.

David's behavior in this story is clearly reprehensible by any moral standard that we as Christians would recognize. Adultery, rape, lying, and multiple murders to silence a witness reflects the possibility of evil of which we are all capable. Christian commitments, of course, call for far more than the avoidance of evil. Discipleship summons us to speaking truthfully as a matter of course,

"The writer has cut very, very deep into the strange web of foolishness, fear, and fidelity that comprises the human map. This narrative is more than we want to know about David and more than we can bear to understand about ourselves."— Brueggemann, *First and Second Samuel*, Interpretation, 27?

to a generosity toward others that places our power in Christ in the service of healing, help, thoughtful care, and constructive kindness. It calls us to practice fidelity in our personal and public lives. That means going beyond avoiding adultery to the creative work of keeping marriage vows. It means keeping promises and commitments when they are made, implications included, without hedging or keeping the letter of requirement without the spirit of intent. It means treating no one like property or objects for our use to satisfy our needs. Instead, in Christ, women, men, and children we know, meet, or pass on the street are subjects of God's love and thereby bound to us in love for love. The story of David and Bathsheba reminds us of our high calling in Christ, which does not impose impossible standards of perfection but offers in Christ a measure for the practice of God's love. Do we do what is right all the time? I certainly don't. But I know in Christ the right to "Love others, as I have loved you." And I am self-deceived if I do not acknowledge the *unlove* I do. Self-deception lies readily at hand for us all. Culture, status, or privilege whispers loudly in our ears that we need to win at all costs, that everybody lies, that cheating is okay if the game is at stake or others are doing it (figuring income taxes is a common example). And we are encouraged to think that we can do as we please with the power and possessions in our control. David took what he wanted with utter disregard for that to which he was most deeply committed: namely, his relationship with God and his service to God's people. If we are honest with ourselves, we know David intimately, do we not?

The outcry of a moral crisis in America in the last years of this millennium has come from all quarters, and the search for causes has resulted in countless theories and opinions. What I notice is that most of them point fingers at some cultural feature—violent television, video games, two-career parents and unsupervised children—or the culture itself, variously called "narcissistic," "secular," "individualistic," "relativistic," and "morally bankrupt." Or they point to the failure of social institutions: the public schools, now stripped of religious symbols and sanctioned rites; political institutions and leadership, which fail to model moral leadership and behavior; or the churches, which have not taken the lead in moral education and development of their own members. Finally, the institution closest to home, the family, is criticized: for neglecting its time-honored role of teaching children right from wrong by both word and example, and for neglecting to develop with them a durable yet adaptable conscience to enable discernment of the right and good thing to do through adolescence and adulthood. No doubt the truth of the matter lies in some multiple combination of all these factors and more. My hope, however, is that in our search to understand moral failure on a public scale, we will look inside ourselves at our own patterns of living, feelings, and impulses, rather than just pointing to larger and more external sources. Perhaps 2 Samuel 11:1–27 can help us take just such account of ourselves in light of our own faith commitments. I hope so.

Want to Know More?

About the Goliath story? See Walter Brueggemann, *First and Second Samuel,* Interpretation (Louisville, Ky.: John Knox Press, 1990), 127–34.

About sojourners in ancient Israel? See Bruce C. Birch, *Let Justice Roll Down: The Old Testament, Ethics, and Christian Life* (Louisville, Ky.: Westminster John Knox Press, 1991), 110–11, 165–66. See also Leland Ryken, James C. Wilhoit, and Tremper Longman III, eds., *Dictionary of Biblical Imagery* (Downers Grove, Ill.: InterVarsity Press, 1998), 300–302.

? Questions for Reflection

1. Why does the Deuteronomic Historian let us see this side of David?
2. How many times in chapter 11 is Uriah's wife referred to by her name—Bathsheba—and how many times is she nameless? Do you think this distinction is important? Why or why not?
3. Uriah was a loyal servant of David and also a "sojourner" in the land. Why is it important that we know these things about him?
4. What recent events in American politics does this passage bring to mind? Do we hold our leaders to a higher moral standard than we hold ourselves?

8

2 Samuel 12:1–15a

David under Judgment

Reading 2 Samuel 11 and 12 back to back, as we are doing, is a reminder that the chapter numbers and divisions were a late afterthought to the composition of the story. Clearly chapter 12 continues the sordid tale of David's lust for Bathsheba, his abuse of her, his adultery, and his murder of Uriah, her husband, in a vain attempt to cover up his paternity of her child. Chapter 12, which is the concern of this unit, brings the destructive events of chapter 11 to closure, its tragic events ultimately but not easily rescued by the grace of God. Without chapter 12, David would appear to get away with his criminal activity. The cover-up afforded by Uriah the Hittite's death in battle might have successfully allowed David to proclaim Uriah the father of Bathsheba's child of rape. With a little imagination, leaning on the earlier story of David's kindness to Mephibosheth, the only surviving member of Saul's family, we can even suppose that the king might have found a very public way to demonstrate his generosity to Bathsheba's child "by Uriah." Current political lingo for that sort of move—the genius of the best political advisors turning loss into gain—is called spin doctoring. David's power and prestige as king surely afforded him ample opportunity for good political moves like the one imagined here. Without chapter 12, David's manipulation of power carries the day, evil triumphs, and the anointed one's obligation to the moral code of the covenant with YHWH becomes a mockery.

As we saw in the last unit, YHWH was surprisingly silent as the events David set in motion by his passion unfolded. Only the narrator's comment at the end reminds us that nothing David has done has escaped notice by God. The totality of David's behavior is summed up in a word: "What David did was evil in YHWH's sight" (11:27, author's translation). Evil is a word in our culture we tend to reserve for events on the scale of the genocide of 6 million Jews during the Holocaust, the wholesale murder of Gypsies during the same period, or the torture and death inflicted by the death squads during El Salvador's civil war in the 1980s. Evil appropriately describes such inhumanity as these atrocities involve. These events and many others are mind-numbing, heart-breaking, and soul-cringing kinds of things that an ordinary person can hardly imagine happening, let alone being personally responsible for. Adultery, political cover-up, lust, even rape and the murder of a single person seem to many to be in another league than "evil" in our culture's vocabulary. These are crimes of passion, we may say, without the calculation and elaborate involvement of the state, as in the other cases noted. Bad, awful, tragic, yes; but is David's behavior and the David-like behavior we recognize in ourselves truly evil? The narrator of David's story does not hesitate for a minute: "What David did was evil in YHWH's sight." Period.

Perhaps our reticence to speak of evil except in extraordinary cases is related to the secularization that characterizes our society and our modern outlook. Sociologists and ethicists in our day have pointed to the lack of agreement among North Americans concerning just what constitutes right and wrong. Robert Bellah and his colleagues, in their widely read book *Habits of the Heart,* point to

> "Terrible as it can be, the worst form of evil is manifested not in natural misfortune that happens to us but in what we human beings do to each other. It appears not in pain, suffering, and death as such, but in the pain, suffering, and death we inflict on each other."—Shirley C. Guthrie, *Christian Doctrine*, rev. ed. (Louisville, Ky.: Westminster John Knox Press, 1994), 173.

how relative right and wrong have become to Americans, each person claiming the right to decide for himself or herself what is right and what is wrong. This kind of "everyone decides for themselves" approach to good and bad behavior tends to shove "evil" into a corner reserved only for the most undeniably heinous events. Holocaust, the slaughter of innocents in war—these kinds of events everyone can quickly agree are "evil." But beyond these, agreement is harder to come by.

Two thoughts to ponder. First, for people of faith especially, evil is a theological word. Like other theological words in a secular society, it seems to have lost its significance for daily life, even for many contemporary believers. Evil describes human defiance of God's love, rebellion of the creature against Creator, and a tearing of the moral fabric of the created order. "Righteousness" and "evil" are relational words in the Bible, describing our relationships with God and, simultaneously, our relationships with others. Righteousness speaks of "right relationship," whole, trustworthy, and loving. Evil, on the other hand, is "broken relationship," destructive, hateful, and false. Evil is a moral word. It represents one end of a continuum of behavior, on the other end of which is "good." For Christians, "good" is living in harmony with God and God's creation.

Evil and good, as moral and religious relational concepts, need a narrative context, a community story. Codes of behavior belong in our Christian tradition within the context of the stories of God's good creation, persistent love, and judgment that is always aimed at restoration and healing. Such a history identifies their transcendent source and remembers a community's history of relationships with one another, with others outside the community, and ultimately with the Holy Other, to whom the community and its members are morally accountable. Given these dynamics, clearly evil and good are morally complex and ambiguous concepts. Knowing what to do that is in harmony with Christian faith and practice requires discernment more than deduction, imagination beyond the observable, and community work to interpret its history of life together. As religion has become in our culture ever more privatized, evil and good have accompanied the move away from the public square. Thus all of us know that evil happens daily and persistently, yet we do not talk about it by that name in public conversation, unless we can find no other word to capture the magnitude of destruction involved. The foreshortening of our public vocabulary by the loss of evil (and good) as relevant religious topics is a costly loss to our social and personal well-being.

What images does the word "evil" bring to mind?

By contrast, modern thought (since the 16th century) is accustomed to looking for reasonable, detectable cause-and-effect relationships between events in human history; and "evil" is not a rational concept lending itself to rational explanation for events. On the contrary, "evil" is how we described what to us is irrational, incomprehensible, and without satisfactory explanation. Evil, in modern parlance, as martyred German theologian and pastor Dietrich Bonhoeffer might have put it, is a word for the "gaps," for the spaces in our experience that defy rational explanation and call for some extraordinary explanation. Modern societies examine human individual and social behavior with the same zeal for cause-and-effect explanations that scientific analysis has exercised in what we have come to call "the natural sciences." This approach has provided important and useful knowledge for all of us, resulting in better medical and psychological care, better understanding of factors involved in criminal behavior, and the potential at least for better government, social structures, and quality of life. We have grown to recognize and appreciate the complexities of cause and effect in human behavior, making simple answers and solutions to human and social problems no longer acceptable.

The risk is always present that the reasons for behavior the human sciences have uncovered can become excuses for behavior that is irresponsible and destructive. In a magazine interview, Hillary Clinton tried to explain her husband's sexual misconduct and spoke of his difficult childhood and other factors that needed, in her view, to be considered. She made it quite clear that she was not making any excuses for him or offering any justification for his behavior. Nevertheless, critics instantly jumped on the interview as doing just that—offering excuses and ducking responsibility.

But a thoughtful radio commentator used the opportunity to invite listeners to consider something of benefit to all of us. He invited us to pay more attention to distinguishing in our own actions, as well as in the actions of others, between offering an explanation of why things seem to happen the way they do, while at the same time stepping up to own responsibility for our behavior. He was urging his audience to recognize the tendency we all have of confusing "excuses" and "explanations." Excuses effectively remove responsibility for actions from the person or group involved and trace the cause to something or someone else. This, he argued, had not been Ms. Clinton's purpose. On the other hand, she had been eager to offer an explanation that could correctly allow consideration of the complicated web of factors—social, familial, and personal—that are interwoven in anyone's decision making and actions, without denying the actor's responsibility for them. The unacceptable alternative is continuing to follow the more common path of either excusing behavior by tracing its cause to events beyond our control or blaming people without any sensitivity to what may have influenced the path they took.

In the case of David's actions so graphically depicted in chapter 11, as modern readers we can find numerous explanations for his behavior in an effort to understand it. It is important, in fact, that we do so. We have seen that David's treatment of Bathsheba and Uriah is "out of character" for him as our writer has drawn the king's portrait. The narrative structure artfully makes a profound point for us. By the end of chapter 11 we are clear: David is not the morally blameless and constantly faithful person we had thought. Or at least that is not *all* he is or is capable of being. The fullness of his character includes heavy, ominous tones and cruel texture *along with* the brighter, luminescent, and triumphant textures so familiar. Such a complex mix of tones and textures, indeed, describes the human palette of moral possibilities. Lest we see in David a case of "good gone bad," we are reminded by his story that good and bad, faithfulness and betrayal, righteousness and evil, lie close at hand in each of us. We harbor within impulses for both good and evil, together with the freedom to decide which inclination to follow. David chose to do evil in this case; but that is not the end of the story, as we are seeing. We too, like David, on occasion choose to do things that are evil from God's point of view; but, like David, we also may choose to do good. Therein lies our hope for renewal. In a significant sense we were right to think David's disregard for the lives of Bathsheba and Uriah was "out of character" for him, just as our hurtful and destructive behavior is out of character for us. Both are "out of character" in the sense that the Bible affirms that the fullness of who we are—our true character, if you will—is found in relationships of love, with God and our companions in creation. Evil abandons love and destroys relationships, dehumanizing those hurt and the evildoer as well. In this sense, we are "out of character" as children of God when we choose to do evil rather than good. But what does it take to confront the evil we do and to repair the torn relationships that have resulted? Chapter 12 offers us wisdom in this regard.

Once again the prophet Nathan enters the story. We remember him from the report in chapter 7 of his vision of God's word to David, promising the king a "house forever" and a relationship of steadfast love with God. By his appearance here, the writer

"Nathan's is the most famous parable in the Old Testament. Like many of the parables of Jesus, it was told in order to get the listener to judge himself. Jesus told so many parables that his listeners came to expect them, and knew that he did not mean them literally; but the effectiveness of Nathan's parable lay precisely in this, that David was fooled into thinking that the prophet was telling him about a real life incident."—Payne, *I & II Samuel*, Daily Study Bible, 208.

encourages us to keep in mind the grace of God, shown so marvelously to David in chapter 7, as chapter 12 unfolds. On another level, Nathan appears before the king because he has been "sent" to speak for YHWH. From the close of chapter 11, we know before he opens his mouth what he has to say to the king. In YHWH's sight, what David has done is evil; Nathan has been sent to bring that devastating word of judgment against him. Nathan is the means by which YHWH will vent his anger toward David, and Nathan is the one who must pronounce God's rendering of consequences for the king's sad choices freely made. All David's efforts at cover-up are at stake in the prophet's confrontation with him on behalf of God's word. What David thought so well hidden has not been hidden at all from the view of the One whose relationship with him means the most.

As Brueggemann suggests, this is a critical and dangerous moment for prophet and king (Brueggemann, 280). As the bearer of God's judgment against David, Nathan risks the wrath of a king who has already demonstrated his willingness to buy silence with murder. Nathan's last word with the king (chapter 7), however, declared God's everlasting love for David and his family. We can imagine David listening attentively to the prophet's word hoping it may be like last time, that somehow the "matter" of Bathsheba and her husband, Uriah, is not what Nathan has come to talk about. Moreover, David listens because he must; he dare not do otherwise because at heart he knows that no matter his power as king, he is first and foremost God's anointed and the shepherd of God's people. While he may have been seduced by his own royal power, David is not so self-absorbed as to doubt the reality of God's power. He is, after all, successor to King Saul, whom YHWH rejected and stripped of his anointing. If David dared believe the promise of steadfast love in relationship with God, then he dared not treat empty the promise made in the same breath of discipline and punishment when evil is done (see 2 Sam. 7:14).

Perhaps the best-known portion of this story is Nathan's parable in verses 1–4. Earlier YHWH communicated to Nathan through a nighttime vision or dream; now Nathan speaks to David in a parable that intends to make a way for God's word in the judgment speech that will follow in verses 7–14. Some commentators have suggested that Nathan's use of a parable to approach the king with such a message so potentially dangerous to the messenger reflects prophetic caution in the face of royal power. Nathan, in other words, gains some time and the sympathy of the king with the parable before he announces the harsh word of YHWH that he bears.

At the same time, we might consider Nathan's use of a parable in these circumstances from another point of view. To be clear, the parable is not part of the message but a means to opening David's eyes and ears to see and hear the truth YHWH has to speak to him. Parables, as rhetorical and literary devices, are always means to some other end; they always point away from themselves to something true that they make more visible and imaginable. To borrow from the imagery of theologian Paul Tillich, parables participate in the truth that they show us, but they are by no means the whole of it; they stand as symbols to truth and a symbolic way into knowing truthfully. Parables as art more generally raise the level of conversation above the rational and literal to the imaginative and descriptive. They help hearers and readers see and hear what is otherwise stuck in the confusion of limited experience, beyond which it is hard for us to see. Parables may help those blind to themselves to see truth that is buried under the weight of denial, shame, fear, or pride. Nathan's parable shakes David's imagination—it forces him to see human injustice and malice so forcefully that his defenses are brought down and his soul opened to empty itself of anger and compassion on behalf of someone so wronged as the poor man in the parable. In seeing the loathsome behavior of the rich man, who had "no pity" (v. 6), David becomes transparent to his own. In rendering judgment against the rich man, David opens himself internally to hear the judgment YHWH has against him. By this parable, Nathan shows David a picture of himself, something on the order of a moral X-ray.

"In the royal narrative of chapter 11 and the prophetic verdict of chapter 12, the text juxtaposes these two views of historical reality. David has been seduced by the royal view; the king now is shown to be answerable to the covenantal prophetic reality, which he cannot escape."— Brueggemann, *First and Second Samuel*, Interpretation, 281.

For us such parables come, I think, often in the form of television scenes of events from which we cannot look away, through which our own prejudices and hates suddenly loom in front of us. One recent event may serve to illustrate. In October 1998, Wyoming college student Matthew Shepard was brutally murdered. He was tied to a fence post, beaten nearly to death, and left to die. When he was found hours later he was taken to a hospital, but he never regained consciousness. The apparent reason for the attack on him: He was gay. As the horror of that tragedy unfolded before us in graphic pictures and chilling descriptions, many of us were forced to confront our own homophobia and latent hate for gay, lesbian, and transgendered people. We were outraged, as David was. We were moved to sincere compassion, as David was, as Matthew Shepard's father and mother struggled to find words to describe their terrible loss. Matthew Shepard's death took place far from most of us, yet it dug deeply at the wounded souls of many of us. There are other media besides television that act as parables for us today: Movies, books, plays, and music all have the power to open us to see around and within ourselves more deeply than otherwise we can or dare, not unlike the way Nathan's parable worked to open David to the word of judgment to come.

With David's outrage poured out and his royal judgment pronounced, the anonymous rich man of the parable is named (vv. 5–7). David's verdict names him "the man deserving death," literally and dramatically "a son of death" and "the man without pity." Nathan, however, boldly declares the evildoer's true identity to David in two unforgettable Hebrew words: "You are the man!" (v. 7). David's shock must have been palpable and likely visible. Consider yourself in the same position and just imagine the moment: blood flushing the face, jaw clenched, palms beginning to sweat, and mind swirling with thought and emotion. David cannot escape YHWH's judging word now. David is now facing the Holy One who has loved him so generously, whose kindness and loyalty he has met with betrayal, violating his relationship with God with the rape of Bathsheba and the murder of Uriah. There is no place to hide either from God or his own self-deception.

The formal pattern of the judgment speech in which Nathan forms God's word against David (vv. 7–12) recurs throughout the prophetic literature of the Bible. It is "stock and trade" in prophetic speech. That does not deny its uniqueness here; but recognizing its formal style helps us understand it better. The judgment speech is trial language, and here it is even foreshadowed in David's outraged speech rendering judgment against the rich man of the parable. David indicts the rich man for particular crimes, pronounces the verdict against him, and renders his punishment (see especially vv. 5–6). The rich man's case was heard in the royal court, with David as accuser and judge, appealing to the covenant moral standards expressed in *Torah*. In David's case, the court is that of YHWH. The familiar words "Thus says YHWH, the God of Israel" identify unmistakably the One adjudicating the charges against David, not unlike a bailiff announcing the trial judge's name at the opening of each session. In the prophetic speech, YHWH is both accuser and judge. "Thus says YHWH" gives way to testimony concerning God's past generosity toward David and the extraordinary comment that, if David had wanted more from YHWH, it would have been granted him. Against this testimony of goodness toward him, YHWH brings the charges (vv. 9–10). David stands accused of "despising the word of YHWH" by doing "evil in [YHWH's] sight," (v. 9). Evidence of his guilt is presented by YHWH's testimony citing David's adultery with Bathsheba, Uriah's wife, and his murder of Uriah in an effort to hide the crime. Judgment is rendered by YHWH quickly: Having killed Uriah by the sword, even if at the hands of the enemy, violence and warfare has entered the marrow of David's household and will not be satisfied until Israel is finally in exile and its throne dismantled. David's secret is uncovered and the public humiliation he sought to avoid he will suffer at the hands of Absalom, his son, the "neighbor" of verse 11, who will claim his father's wives during an attempted coup d'état (2 Samuel 16).

> "The parable does its powerful work. David's response is immediate, indignant, and on target. David is properly appalled at the crassness of the rich man who acts in ways that are economically and sexually destructive. The rich man receives a harsh royal indictment (v. 5). The king, accustomed to conducting judicial procedure, indicts and sentences (cf. 15:1–6). Death is in order. Reparation must be made."—Brueggemann, *First and Second Samuel*, Interpretation, 280.

Before Nathan has finished, David speaks two words to parallel Nathan's two that declared "You are the man." If Nathan's are life-threatening words, David's words are life seeking: they are his confession. "I have sinned against YHWH." No excuses. These are critical words for bearing responsibility and thus opening the way for forgiveness, healing, restoration, and a new beginning to life, though one forever changed by the encounter with God and self. David's confession will save his life, since, even more than the rich man of the parable, he fairly deserves to die for his crimes.

It is mind-boggling to us to move so rapidly from the outrage of divine indictment and judgment to Nathan's declaration, "YHWH has already taken away your sin, you shall not die" (v. 13, author's translation). Confession and forgiveness in the same verse. That his sin has been graciously taken away, however, does not stay the consequences of David's behavior. God's words of judgment stand, and death and suffering have entered David's household with the same surety of "forever" that accompanied the promises of chapter 7. (NRSV's "shall never depart" in verse 10 includes the same Hebrew expression "forever" that we saw in chapter 7.) There is no cheap forgiveness here; on the contrary, the cost is high not only to David but also to all those around him and ahead of him in time.

The last word in our passage begins the lethal road David's sin has paved; the child born of lust, rape, and murder will not survive (v. 14). We miss the point, I think, if we take this word as crude justice, the child's life substituting for David's. A child's death is horrible to us, and rightly we struggle with any suggestion that God consigned Bathsheba's child to death to assuage David's sin. The Abraham and Isaac story stands as a barrier against attributing child sacrifice to the delight and satisfaction of Israel's God. We stand closer to the truth, I think, both ancient and modern if we see in this anticipated tragedy a graphic statement of the infection in David's personal and public life let loose by his evil behavior.

The story means to work on us in at least two profound ways. First, it means to trouble us, disturb us, and ultimately forces us to self-examination regarding how what we have done and do breaks and destroys and harms—the evidences of evil in God's sight. Second, it means to urge us to confession, to taking responsibility for our actions that violate the law of love incarnate in the Word of God who is Jesus Christ. Confession begins the road to personal and communal change and transformation; it is not a perfunctory moment in our Sunday worship, though it may seem so, but a radical step toward new life. The dramatic instant in which David's confession becomes Nathan's announcement of God's forgiveness is a beacon for us,

Want to Know More?

About parables? See William Barclay, *The Parables of Jesus* (Louisville, Ky.: Westminster John Knox Press, 1999), and Robert Stein, *An Introduction to the Parables of Jesus* (Philadelphia: Westminster Press, 1981).

About prophetic speech? See James D. Newsome, Jr., *The Hebrew Prophets* (Atlanta: John Knox Press, 1984), 1–15. For a more detailed discussion, see either Ronald E. Clements, *Old Testament Prophecy: From Oracles to Canon* (Louisville, Ky.: Westminster John Knox Press, 1996), or Joseph Blenkinsopp, *A History of Prophecy in Israel,* revised and enlarged edition (Louisville, Ky.: Westminster John Knox Press, 1996).

About the sources of evil? See Shirley C. Guthrie, *Christian Doctrine,* rev. ed. (Louisville, Ky.: Westminster John Knox Press, 1994), 166–91; Tyron L. Inbody, *The Transforming God: An Interpretation of Suffering and Evil* (Louisville, Ky.: Westminster John Knox Press, 1997).

too. The One whose goodness demands our confession is just that eager to forgive and pave the way for a change of heart and behavior over and over again in each of us.

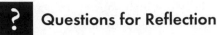 **Questions for Reflection**

1. Do you think the word "evil" is too strong to use as a label for David's actions in chapter 11? Why or why not?
2. What are some events in the news today that you would characterize as "evil"?
3. Walter Brueggemann writes that the telling of the parable is a "high-risk moment" for both prophet and king. What is at risk for Nathan? What is at risk for David?
4. Despite his sins and his failure to confess them until the last minute, God forgives David without hesitation. What does this say about God's love for God's children?

2 Samuel 18:9–19:8

9

David and Absalom at War

We are nearing the end of our journey through 1 and 2 Samuel. But we cannot finish this study without hearing and reflecting upon one of the most painful stories in the two volumes. The grief unleashed within David's family as a consequence of his adultery with Bathsheba and the murder of her husband, Uriah, has cast a pall over David and his children. In the chapters that follow David's confession and reconciliation with YHWH in chapter 12, family crisis, pain, and distress are unrelenting. The figure who stands either center stage or not far in the background throughout is David's son, Absalom. Pathos in David's family reaches its highest point, in David's view and that of the narrative, with Absalom's death at the hands of his father's general, Joab. The overwhelming grief of David is carried on one of the Bible's most unforgettable laments: "O my son Absalom, my son, my son Absalom! Would I had died instead of you, O Absalom, my son, my son!" (18:33).

None of us, as parents or children of parents, can read this story of Absalom's armed rebellion against his father, and David's involvement in his son's death, without being emotionally touched and caught up in the grief of the account. The distance between us and David's story, in time, space, and political status, fades away, drowned out by the terrible grief of a father for a lost child and an irreparably broken parental relationship. As we try to understand the narrative of this unit and look for meanings for ourselves, I suspect we will find ourselves starting close to home, within our families. That, I think, is what the writer of this scripture hopes will happen.

A synopsis of the narrative from chapter 12 to chapter 18 may help bring us to the moment of tragic climax in our passage. Each of the intervening scenes is worth more detailed attention than possible in this ten-unit study. Yet none of them—nor the passage of our unit—stands alone. It is important to remind ourselves constantly that they are part of a whole narrative history, the point of which is never entirely visible until its end in 2 Kings 25:29. The national and personal grief and disorientation rising as lament to God and threatening Israel's identity forever is prefigured in the catastrophe of David's family and the inheritance it becomes to each subsequent generation. Hopefully your future studies will take you closer to the Deuteronomic Historian's closing scenes. For now, we must risk focusing on only a part of the whole, gleaning its meaning for us while humbly remembering that this is not all there is to it. We may not forget what a bold claim we Christians make when we say that a portion of our scripture provides insight from God into our reality when it is read and heard in light of the whole biblical narrative.

The key verse in the David story that sets the tone and direction for all that happens after chapter 12 is this: "Thus says YHWH, 'I am raising against you evil from within your own family'" (12:11a, author's translation). What about Nathan's subsequent affirmation, when David has confessed to his sin, that YHWH has "already passed over your sin" (12:13, author's translation)? Does that not mean that the promised evil (NRSV's "trouble" does not carry the weight of the judgment of YHWH) ought to be averted in the story? As I mentioned in the last unit, the narrator knows the truth about what we think and do. Forgiven though we may be upon confession, the consequences of our actions cannot be recalled but flow undeniably forth from us toward others and the future. David is forgiven, yes; but the violence wrought by his hand is not easily stayed. David does not have the moral strength within his own family to do it.

That may be the greatest tragedy of this sad story, but it is a circumstance to which we can relate readily. If we look into the history of our families, we may not be surprised to find some significant event in the past in the life of one person or couple that has subsequently flooded over and colored their heirs generation after generation, right to us. Perhaps the stream has slowed but traces may still be seen, and the wear and tear on the family fabric may still be evident. I can think of examples along the limbs of my family tree, and I imagine many of you can, too. Evil, pain, suffering, and destruction such as David set loose travels subversively through subsequent generations. Hope for altering the flow of historical consequence lies in recognition of its reality in the present and a conscious resistance and reshaping of it into the future. Change such as this requires faith, moral courage, and moral vigilance. David seemed blessed with a loyal and steadfast faith, possessing the gifts of moral courage and vigilance in far less measure.

The reach across generations of one person's ambition and unconscionable behavior is the burden of William Faulkner's epic 1936 novel, *Absalom, Absalom!* (New York: Random House, 1993). Faulkner's central character is Thomas Sutpen, a man obsessed with establishing a family dynasty as a means to the larger purpose of gaining entry into the aristocratic plantation culture of the pre–Civil War South. Sutpen, like David, is a "taker" in the story, though unlike David he has no moment of confession—only regret when one scheme after another fails to accomplish his desires. The novel spans the years 1807 to 1910, four generations of the Sutpen family. In the end, Thomas Sutpen's

William Faulkner

desire for admission to the southern culture, so steeped in tradition and mystique, comes to nothing except a tragic road upon which all those who come in contact with him must walk. The sole surviving heir of Thomas Sutpen, when the novel closes, is a great-grandson. He is a nearly mindless young man who has disappeared into the woods of Sutpen's would-be plantation. He is the symbol of the impossibility of Sutpen's grand yet ill-conceived design to create a past for himself that never existed and a future for his name that he can control.

With his choice of title, Faulkner has connected his story of a family tragedy set loose in one generation and reverberating through the future of three more to the David story. It carries us, specifically, to the anguished outcry of David the parent for his lifeless son and for a future that now never can be. Though a world of difference separates Thomas Sutpen from David, they share the tragedy, grief, and suffering that arise from the embers of passionate and selfish desire and quickly swirl out of control, consuming even those with whom they are most intimate. David's taking of Bathsheba has the effect of Sutpen's "grand design," as he calls it. This "grand design" ends in a blazing inferno that takes the lives of his son and a granddaughter. Faulkner's image is most fitting. David's story moves beyond Absalom to Solomon, Bathsheba's child. But violence and deceit are enthroned with him and continue to plague David's house well beyond David's death.

"It seems that this demon—his name was Sutpen . . . Colonel Sutpen. Who came out of nowhere and without warning upon the land with a band of strange niggers and built a plantation—(Tore violently a plantation, Miss Rosa Coldfield says). . . . And married her sister Ellen and begot a son and a daughter which—(Without gentleness begot, Miss Rosa Coldfield says). . . . Which should have been the jewels of his pride and the shield and comfort of his old age, only—(Only they destroyed him or something or he destroyed them or something. And died)—and died."—William Faulkner, *Absalom, Absalom!* (New York: Random House, 1993), 3.

The story of David's family, as the narrative has shaped it, involves only a select number of David's children. Second Samuel 3:2 provides a list of the sons and daughters born to David in Hebron, and 5:13 those born to him in Jerusalem. Of all these children, the narrative pursues the lives of only five: Amnon, the first born; Tamar, his half-sister; Absalom, second in line for the throne; Adonijah; and Solomon. Eventually, as we know, Solomon became king and his reign powerfully shaped the life and culture of Israel. The Deuteronomic writer sums up this reign as "idolatrous," far from the model of his faithful father, David (see 1 Kings 11:1–9). Since succession to the throne in Israel was ordinarily by order of birth, the obvious historical question playing in the background of David's family story is this: How did Solomon, at best fourth in line, become king instead of any of David's first three sons? However, the primary theological concern in the narrative is with David and his faithfulness to YHWH—the one quality of character he has shown throughout, albeit tragically bracketed for a decisive moment when lust reigned instead. David's passion for YHWH does not govern his behavior without exception, but that passion and that commitment are nonetheless constantly part of David's being. That makes confession and renewal possible for him, as we have seen.

Chapter 13 tells of the horrible rape of Tamar by her half-brother, Amnon. (For a powerful interpretation of this narrative see Trible, 37–63.) The story is told in ways that make unmistakable connection to David's abuse of Bathsheba. Amnon's lust leaves Tamar humiliated, her future in shambles. Amnon, finished with her, throws her out for public display. David, we are told, "became very angry, but he would not punish his son Amnon, because he loved him, for he was his firstborn" (13:21). Absalom, Tamar's brother, is not so generous. He takes justice into his own hands and organizes a conspiracy that results in the assassination of his brother Amnon. Chapter 13 closes with Absalom in flight, a fugitive from his father and a refugee in Geshur.

After three years, David allows Absalom to return to Jerusalem, though he is confined to his own quarters and forbidden to approach the king (14:1–24). Two years later, Absalom seeks freedom

> ### David's Children
> The sons born to David in Hebron (2 Samuel 3:2) were, in birth order: Amnon, Chileab, Absalom, Adonijah, Shephatiah, and Ithream. The sons and daughters born to him in Jerusalem (2 Samuel 5:13) were Shammua, Shobab, Nathan, Solomon, Ibhar, Elishua, Nepheg, Japhia, Elishama, Eliada, and Eliphelet.

from his house arrest by throwing himself on his father's mercy. In a verse wonderful for its powerful compression, chapter 14 concludes: "So he came to the king and prostrated himself with his face to the ground before the king; and the king kissed Absalom" (14:33).

David forgives, but Absalom has had a long time to store up animosity toward his father. He sets a course to usurp the throne, stirring up popular displeasure with the king's failure to establish a working judicial system in Jerusalem (15:1–6). In the end, the narrator tells us, "he stole the hearts of the people of Israel" (15:6). The conspiracy continues to grow with a number of David's trusted officials and the majority of the people casting their lot with Absalom and against the king until David is forced out of Jerusalem, leaving the city and his concubines to Absalom's will (15:7–18). David's military force apparently consisted of little more than the court guard. The priests, Zadok and Abiathar, remain loyal to him, a sign of his faithfulness before YHWH, as does the advisor Hushai. From this point forward to chapter 18, the narrative concerns preparations for a military showdown between father and son.

Walter Brueggemann is very helpful when we try to visualize this compressed account of events that no doubt took some time to unfold. David's departure from Jerusalem is not panicked retreat. "This narrative pattern," Brueggemann writes, "may be intended like a passion narrative, in which David is headed for his 'wilderness,' but the narrative takes time for important business to be conducted along the way" (Brueggemann, 302). The one who came from the wilderness tending sheep to become king, who lived in the wilderness as a fugitive from King Saul, finally emerging to claim the throne in

Jerusalem, must now return the way he has come, facing Saulide opponents who curse and mock him as he goes. But he also gathers support and builds a strategy for winning back the throne even as he is departing the city.

Here the character of David is laid open before us. He loves well but not wisely; he is a person of abiding faith and commitment to YHWH who is willing to stake his return to Jerusalem on YHWH's will. But he is also a realistic politician, laying plans that may be, God willing, the means for putting down his son's coup d'état. The theological statement woven into the story of David's retreat from Jerusalem in the face of Absalom's rebellion is important for us. David must struggle with the political realities he faces, and he must do so as a person of faith and as a father as well.

The narrator of the story of Absalom's rebellion allows questions to arise for readers concerning how YHWH is involved in all that is going on. Truly the writer's hand is not heavy in this regard. Chapter 12 marks the last place where, by way of the prophet Nathan, we are privy to YHWH's perspective on David's life and deeds. No divine intervention stays the hand of Amnon to save Tamar from his lust, and no divine force stops Absalom from avenging her by taking Amnon's life savagely. By the time readers absorb the shock of David's departing Jerusalem for apparent exile, the question of God's intent can hardly be avoided. What is becoming of YHWH's intent toward this man whom YHWH chose to be king, promising him an everlasting dynasty?

Part of what makes these narratives involving David and his family seem so realistic, even to us, may be found in the writer's restraint with regard to YHWH's role in all of it. In the case of David and Absalom, God's purpose is worked out through the agency of the people involved. These include David's priests, who remain in Jerusalem as espionage agents; their sons, who serve as messengers to David; an unnamed woman, who protects the spies from Absalom's men; and a "plant" in the council of Absalom who is loyal to David, named Hushai. Brueggemann points to what he calls "one of the key verses of Samuel" (Brueggemann, 313) for a clue to YHWH's role in the events taking place. When Ahithophel, one of David's advisors whose word was described as "the word of God" (2 Sam. 16:23), defected to Absalom, David prayed, "O YHWH, I ask you, turn the counsel of Ahithophel into foolishness" (15:31). With modest hope, David left Hushai in Jerusalem to try to counter the advice of Ahithophel. In a crucial moment, Hushai's proffered strategy to Absalom, fantastic and impractical militarily, is accepted by the rebel. In that crucial moment, the narrator explains everything: Hushai's wild plan is accepted instead of Ahithophel's more practical and logical one because "YHWH had ordained to defeat the good counsel of Ahithophel, so that YHWH might bring Absalom to ruin" (17:14, author's translation). David's prayer is answered. "God," Brueggemann notes, "is utterly partisan to David" (Brueggemann, 313). Before the battle with Absalom begins, readers know the outcome. Absalom is doomed to certain defeat; David is still God's choice as king over God's people.

With the opening of chapter 18 we move to David's preparations for battle with his son, a most unnatural enemy. Militarily, Absalom's grave mistake may have been driving David into the field, where his strength as a leader had always been at its best. That is evident here in 18:1–8, as David prepares his forces for the field. Unlike Absalom's troops, who march under one commanding general, David has divided his forces under three commanders: the long trusted and loyal Joab; Ittai the Gittite, a foreigner who joined David along the way; and Abishai, Joab's brother. Preparations at last over, the narrative carries us to the moment of battle. The king, persuaded to stay in the city for his own safety and the sake of the troops who would be forced to protect him in the field, takes a last moment to address his officers, within earshot of the troops. What he says is both touching and crucial to the story of Absalom's death. In 18.5, David's last thought as the troops leave is about Absalom. He orders his leaders, "Deal gently for my sake with the young man Absalom." The coup must be put down, David knows; but somehow he hopes to salvage the chief traitor, his own son, from the punishment usually afforded those at the center of a coup. Death is what, by all standards of justice, Absalom deserves; but David pleads for personal privilege in this case. "Deal gently for my sake with the young man Absalom."

Lengthy preparations are overwhelmed by the speed with which the outcome of the battle is recounted (18:1–8). Absalom's troops are completely routed, though they seemed to

> "There are few narrative episodes concerning David that are more carefully wrought than this, or more poignantly expressed. The commanders of David must win, but they must 'deal gently' with Absalom. The last sound in their ears is the lingering word of David: 'Deal gently' (18:5)."—Brueggemann, *First and Second Samuel*, Interpretation, 318.

be the superior force. YHWH's favor toward David, though unspoken here, is no doubt behind the surprising but complete victory of

David's troops. The last line in the account, verse 8, particularly tells the tale. "The battle spread over the face of the whole country; and the forest claimed more victims that day than the sword." I asked my neighbor, a man of military training and experience, how he would understand this verse. He described combat at close quarters in thick, wooded forest on uneven ground. It is an easy place to lose one's bearings, to be easily trapped and an easy target for an enemy momentarily free. It is, he said, a deadly place for confusion and death at the hands of one's own troops, what we today would call "friendly fire." Sadly, I thought of Vietnam's jungles and the night attacks during the Gulf War, both settings that left troops vulnerable to attack and self-destruction.

The culmination of the entire narrative is now before us. David has won, but what of Absalom? The cryptic note about the dense forest provides the transition to personal tragedy for him. The end is quickly told in 18:9–18. Absalom, riding through the woods, is suddenly snatched from his mule when his long hair (see 14:26 for comment on Absalom's hair) catches in the branches of an oak tree. He is left hanging, the narrator says provocatively, "between heaven and earth," an ambiguity Joab would shortly dissolve. He is spotted by one of David's men and the news of his entrapment is reported to Joab, whose loyalty to David has obsessed him with complete victory and protection of the king. To that end, he does not hesitate to do his duty as he sees it, killing the helpless Absalom himself (18:4). Now the trumpet can be sounded and the battle declared a victory. But the terrible task of reporting the news to David remains, and that occupies verses 19–32 of chapter 18.

"Would I had died instead of you, O Absalom, my son, my son!"—2 Sam. 18:33

Joab wisely knows that there is great danger is carrying this news to David. The news of the victory will be well received. But to speak of Absalom's death in the face of the final command of David to deal with him "gently for my sake," opens the messenger to the full wrath of the king and the real possibility of the messenger's death. David has done as much before, in the case of the messengers who came to tell him of Saul and Jonathan's deaths. The narrator draws out the scene that finally brings two messengers before David, letting our anxiety stir. One of them, the son of David's priest, loses his courage at the moment of truth (18:28–29). But the dangerous truth must be told. To David's persistent question, "Is it well with the young man Absalom?" the second messenger responds, "May the enemies of my lord the king, and all who rise up to do you harm, be like that young man" (18:32). The narrative grows tense in anticipation of David's response. But it is not wrath or threat but full-throated, unguarded, and undiminished grief sounded on the repeated wailing of the king, "My son, my son Absalom! Would I had died instead of you, O Absalom, my son, my son!" (18:33). In David's heart, there is no room for victory celebration over his enemy son; there is only brokenness and raw pain. It is Joab, again, who finally penetrates David's sorrow long enough to remind him of his responsibilities as king and the imminent danger he is in of losing the loyalty of his followers and potentially the throne (19:5–8). David is not free, as king, to mourn so loudly or inconsolably. He must get on with the job of governance, heart heavy or not; he must get on with his life, though he will never be the same.

Absalom became, by his own choice, his father's unnatural enemy; David, forced to violence against his son, tried to moderate the outcome with a plea: "deal gently." But when the time came he was powerless to save his son's life. It is an agonizing story for us to hear, because we know so personally the pain of broken relationships and enmity within our own families, with our own sons and daughters, mothers and fathers. Jesus teaches us, "Love your enemies, and pray for those who persecute you" (Matt. 5:44). How hard that is to do! Most of the time, it remains abstract for us; that's how we can live with it best, when "enemies" remain faceless and generic. The story of David and Absalom, however, is a story that invites us to think very concretely and personally about loving enemies, by forcing us to look at enmity that lives within our own families. There is no doubt that David loved Absalom. His anguish at his death cries

📖 **Want to Know More?**

About the making of monuments in Old Testament times? See George Arthur Buttrick, ed., *The Interpreter's Dictionary of the Bible*, vol. K–Q (Nashville: Abingdon Press, 1962), 815–17.

About the differences between the Hebrew text of the Bible and our modern English translations? See Bruce M. Metzger and Roland E. Murphy, eds., *The New Oxford Annotated Bible with the Apocrypha*, New Revised Standard Version (New York: Oxford University Press, 1991), xxi–xxiii.

out that he loved him to the end, even when the son took the field determined to destroy his father. By contrast, Absalom shows little trace of love for his father; he is full of rage, bitterness, and staggering ambition to be king.

How do you love your enemy when the enemy is your son? How do you do that on the field of everyday life, with all its uncertainties, responsibilities, and decisions of others that are out of your control? The dramatic level of David's story brings us to full attention regarding our own commitment to love our enemies before Christ. Our enemies are children of God, as we are, all belonging to a single loving parent who knows the enmity of children like us and overcomes our hate with love time after time. The David and Absalom story provides clues between the lines that may help us practice loving our enemies. Let me close by pointing to three:

- David demonstrates careful thought and patience as he withdraws from Jerusalem, knowing all that is at stake with Absalom. Enemy love calls for that kind of patience and deliberate, thoughtful action.

- No doubt David knows he must defeat the coup that Absalom has led, yet he begs for "dealing gently" with his son, searching, as we might put it, for a way to transform the situation into a "win-win" outcome. Sadly, he fails; but the clue for us is genuine.

- Enemy love is risky and potentially destructive to both enemy and lover. David has no choice, since political threat and parent love force it upon him. Ironically, grief seems unavoidable in enemy love, since alienation belongs to both lover and enemy and overcoming it requires giving up familiar ground in mutual relationship. David tries to minimize the destructive risk, especially to Absalom. But he is unsuccessful because matters ultimately are out of his control. Nonetheless, this effort at balancing risk is a matter to take seriously in our practice of enemy love, too.

In the end, the story of David and Absalom, for all we may learn from it, is not a happy story. It is tragic, redeemed only by the grace of God who is persistently present throughout. There is no joy in the death of an enemy, especially one who shares a place with you in family. God in Christ extends beyond our imagination the breadth of family. For us, no enemy falls outside those bounds or our obligation to love them. May David's lament over his son ring in our ears and tear at our hearts, lest we forget just how precious and difficult our calling to love our enemies is in God's sight.

 ## Questions for Reflection

1. In this unit it is said that David "loves well but not wisely." What does that mean? Do you ever feel that you love "well but not wisely"?
2. Look again at the description of "enemy love" in this unit. Why does God ask this of us? Is God asking too much of God's creatures to expect them to love those who do them such harm?
3. Look back at 2 Samuel 12:11–12. Do you think David had any idea that those words of God would come back to haunt him in such a personal way?
4. Twice now David has heard a messenger deliver unhappy news (Nathan in 2 Samuel 12, the Cushite in 2 Sam. 18:32), and both times he has refused to "kill the messenger." Why?

10 | 2 Samuel 22:1–51

A Closing Song of Celebration

We have come to the end of our study of the books of Samuel. Fittingly, we end with a song, joyful music celebrating the saving power of God. We began this journey of faith with another song sung in the face of impossible overcoming. That one was placed on the lips of Hannah, who celebrated boisterously the creation of life out of death visible in the birth of Samuel from a barren womb (1 Samuel 2). This one at the end of the story is placed on the lips of the king whom Hannah's song anticipated—YHWH's chosen and anointed one, David.

Prose cannot adequately convey what our historian wants to say about all that has happened between Hannah's fulfilled emptiness and the closing age of David's reign. In our age, we might say that prose is too left-brained, too linear, too structurally bound. No, the celebration of the moment that the Deuteronomic writer has in mind requires something more imaginative than narrative, something less trapped by time, something like surround-sound or a "home theater" set-up with six speakers arranged to fill the room. Such good news that needs to be told here at the end of Samuel is a *crescendo* that can only be sung on the right-brain chords of poetic imagination. It must be a psalm, a liturgical melody fit for the worship of our God, who "raises up the poor from the dust; he lifts the needy from the ash heap, to make them sit with princes and inherit a seat of honor" (1 Sam. 2:8).

Expressing the power, mystery, and majesty of God and God's indomitable will and steadfast love for Israel and all creation is always limited by the capacity of human speech. Poetry lets us fly to the limits of speech's boundaries and reach for the depths of mystery. Poetry and music together—psaltery or hymnody—increase the dimensions of meaning by uniting body, mind, and soul in storied song in worship in the presence of God.

Recently, the church I attend in Louisville devoted an entire Sunday service to the celebration of hymnody. Liturgical responses, doxologies, hymns of praise, thanksgiving, and confession were all called upon to enable us to express together the inexpressible goodness and grace of our loving, living God. We soared with the music's "Hallelujahs" and probed our hearts and minds with confronting verses and melodies, as if opening our mouths could do no less than pour forth our souls. Of course we, along with other congregations, sing such liturgies every worship service. But what made this Sunday different at our church was consciousness. Our music director urged us to keep in mind as we raised our voices together that we were singing our faith. We were singing the story of God's presence from the beginning with us, from creation to our particular moment in time and space. Our singing songs and prayers and psalms together joined us to the people of God in every age, all of us, as St. Paul puts it, children and heirs of Abraham and Sarah. Our music proclaimed in worship the steadfast presence of God with us and the promise of God's future still ahead of us, urging us into a trustworthy unknown.

The song of 2 Samuel 22:1–51 is music like this. It sings Israel's faith in the context of worship. Thus, though our historian gives David the solo role, the song is unmistakably about the saving and victorious power of Israel's trustworthy and steadfastly loving God. The resounding theme of the psalm, evident in the multiple use of "saving words" that punctuate it, is YHWH's will and power to save those in whom YHWH "delights" (v. 20). While even sharper in Hebrew, English readers can see the concentration of these words in the psalm by simply circling, underlining, or counting them. For example, one word for "deliverance" occurs in verses 1, 18, and 49, while another occurs in verses 2 and 44. A Hebrew word for "save," "savior," or "salvation" occurs in verses 3, 4, 28, 36, 42, 47, and 51!

This information is crucial for us because it indicates that the meaning of David's song truly concerns much more than the title for it in verse 1 would indicate. The song may bring joy to the hearts and lives of all of us for whom "saving words" remain words of gospel and hope. Enslaved Israel cried out to God and God heard their suffering sounds and, for no other reason than God's delight, God rescued the oppressed, delivered them into a land, and made them a people of God. This is the story of Exodus, and Miriam sings wildly of deliverance, in sounds and music not unlike what we are reading (Ex. 15:1–21). Israel became a people by God's rescue, deliverance, and salvation—all themes that are celebrated throughout the First Testament. The Second Testament continues the sounds of salvation, rescue, and grace. The church, like ancient Israel, passes through the waters of salvation in our baptism, joined as rescued people in the body of Christ, our Savior. The church gathers around the table of salvation, set by God in Christ, in the presence of enemies whom Paul calls "principalities and powers." Together we break and eat bread in Christ's name, and enter again into the new covenant offered us by Christ. Thereby "we proclaim the Lord's death until he comes" again and recommit ourselves to a disciple's work of loving justly and walking humbly. To remember St. Paul's words again, "we are being saved" (see 1 Cor. 1:18 or 2:15), holding firmly to our faith. Songs of salvation and rescue, deliverance, and the delight of God are very much melodies we want and need to sing, because they concern us, though not only us.

David's song is our song; and, in a poetic sense, we may replace David's name with our names in verse 1. Of course, the wonder of poetry and music is that whoever's name is on it or whatever event may once have called it out of the depths of soul and mind of an author cannot limit its call on a reader quite distanced from the author's experience. Hearts touched by God and gifted with words to express the moment are unconstrained by time and space and wind their way to give light and sound to experiences of God in our lives, too. To return for a moment to my own experience in worship at my church in Louisville, our congregation has begun over the last few years to respond unprompted with "Amen" after an anthem sung or a sacred dance interpretation offered or the postlude played. The Hebrew root meaning of *amen* is "firmness," "solidity," something to be counted on. Liturgically, we might translate it, "May it be so." The response transforms the music we've heard or the dance witnessed into prayers we all can share, affirmations of our trust in God. Striking to me—apart from what some have seen as the unPresbyterian character of this behavior—has been the spontaneity with which this corporate responding began and continues. It is as if we just could not keep silent in the presence of such poetry of joy, solemnity, or mystery. Second Samuel 22 explodes beyond its own time of creation to create anew in ours. Together, we will find moments to say "amen," I have no doubt; and we will find creative words for songs of praise that long for expression from the bottom of our hearts.

What then shall we say about this psalm as "David's song of the day YHWH delivered him from the hands of his enemies and from the hands of Saul" (v. 1)? The modern mind in us cannot resist the question: "*Did* David compose this song; and are the lyrics his words; and was deliverance from Saul *really* its occasion?" The question we want to ask, however, cannot be answered with certainty. Most scholars hold that the narrative about David that began in 1 Samuel 16, and even far earlier in a veiled way in Hannah's song in 1 Samuel 2, comes to a conclusion in 2 Samuel 20. This chapter connects with 1 Kings 1–2, in which Solomon's succession to his father's throne is dramatically portrayed. Reading 2 Samuel 20 and 1 Kings 1 successively is a good way to see the point. As Brueggemann helpfully points out, these final chapters in 2 Samuel (21–24) are "commonly regarded as a miscellaneous appendix, consisting of materials that are old and have originated at various times but now have been grouped here" (Brueggemann, 335). They are not arranged here in a haphazard fashion, however, but in a very careful structure, with two songs of David at the heart of it (see McCarter, 18–19, for a diagram of the arrangement).

> ### Psalmody vs. Hymnody
>
> For two centuries after the Reformation, followers of John Calvin sang only scriptural songs, mostly metrical versions of the psalms. In the late sixteenth and seventeenth centuries, some English psalters were published that contained a few "hymns of human composition." Over the next two centuries there was much debate over the increase in the singing of hymns as opposed to psalms. By the late nineteenth century many Reformed congregations opted for the use of hymnals rather than psalters. Today, there is renewed interest in psalmody, with more churches using psalters such as *The Psalter: Psalms and Canticles for Singing* (Louisville, Ky.: Westminster John Knox Press, 1993) and *Psalter for Christian Worship* (Louisville, Ky.: Witherspoon Press, 1999).

Because our poem may also be found elsewhere as Psalm 18, it seems likely that "the shapers of Samuel have taken a well-known liturgic piece and placed it here as a concluding theological reflection on the life and faith of David" (Brueggemann, 339). So, while we cannot say who wrote the "song of David" or when, we can say that it may properly be thought of as a song of David in the sense that it is *about* David's faith. Placing this psalm here invites us to think back across the whole story of David's selection by YHWH to serve God as king over all God's people. It asks us to remember his rise to power, his fall to lust, the agony of Absalom's revolt and death, and his victories over enemies that threatened Israel all along the way. But here it is not narrative summary that is of concern but the meaning of David's story for Israel's faith, and, as we read it, for ours. The subject of this psalm, like all those of the psalter, is first and finally God, who is the giver of our faith and the center of our meaning.

The song reverberates in the opening verses (1–4) with sounds and images that remind us of Martin Luther's "A Mighty Fortress Is Our God." The images for God come so rapidly that they pile up. God is rock, fortress, deliverer, a refuge, shield and horn of salvation, stronghold, and savior—all in three verses! Here is a treasury of ways to name God, a treasury that comes offering welcome possibilities to those of us who thirst for language larger than the limited list we too often call upon. These are images of protection, defense, and deliverance from all that threatens to destroy us, all that is arrayed against life and celebrates death.

Most eloquently, our poet lets us see and feel death's threat (vv. 5–6) with images of being overcome, encompassed, and dragged down to the place of the dead, Sheol. The metaphor of a watery grave, with "waves of death" and "torrents of emptiness" (my translation, rather than NRSV's "perdition") drowning him, captures experiences we either know or know about. For a while I served a small church in a fishing village in Maine. Our children were quite young and willing, as I was then, to swim in the cold summer water. Always threatening to me, as a father watching over two boys, were the sudden waves of a passing fishing boat or pleasure craft that rushed toward us, as if trying to catch us unaware and drive us deep below the water. The accompanying threat was the seaweed and kelp in which a foot could easily get entangled, holding a swimmer prisoner, struggling to get free to breathe again. The men who fished those waters were deeply respectful of them, knowing that, while the sea gave them a livelihood, it could easily and summarily take their lives if they failed to stay vigilant while on the water. We use this metaphor ourselves to speak of times of feeling overwhelmed, of drowning, so overcome by daily life that we cannot seem to take a breath or see a way through the murkiness in which we're flailing about. These may be times of extraordinary busyness, demands of home or work all mounting up seemingly at once like waves stirred by some powerful engine not our own. They may be times of deep, overwhelming grief or depression, tears drowning hope and blurring all vision, with no end in sight.

All of us know times in our lives and the lives of others when we feel as if we are surrounded, besieged, at war with enemies of our own naming—and, perhaps, our own making. They may not be Philistines or Saulides, but they are very real to us. The enemies of God's intention for good life for all of us—lives of joy, hope, love, and justice—are "legion" in our day. To seek their names one has only to ask, "What threatens to dull human life? What empties it of meaning and hope? What socially constructed lies about 'happiness,' and 'success' and 'personal wealth' mislead? What do we do to our neighbors, the earth, and ourselves that betrays God's covenant of love?" These enemies, clearly, are never entirely outside ourselves, whether we think individually or about the church. David's enemies may have been "others"; but ours are both beyond our reach and within our personal and corporate patterns of living and making decisions. We need desperately for God, our rock and refuge, our deliverer and defender, to protect us from destructiveness that is apparent in our society, present in our church life, threatening in our neighbor's anger and enmity, and experienced in our own rage, abuse, and self-destructiveness. David knew his enemies; and we must learn to name ours. We dare to do so, only because we can also name God confidently as "my rock, my fortress, and my deliverer" (v. 1).

Drowning and threats against God's desire for life that is whole and complete (the meaning of *shalom*) do not have the last word in David's song, thank God. In the midst of hopelessness and ensnared by death, hope cries to Hope. Verse 7, both simple and rich in structure and language, conveys nonetheless completely the miracle of relationship with our God: "In my distress, I called YHWH; to my God, I cried out. And God heard my voice from the temple" (my translation). In Luther's hymn, a similar thought soars in the third verse: "The prince of darkness grim, we tremble not for him; His rage we can endure, for lo! his doom is sure, One little word shall fell him" (*Presbyterian Hymnal*, 260).

> "This inclusion provides a theological context in which the whole of the literature of I and II Samuel is to be understood. The history of David (and of Israel) is not simply a tale of power and conflict but concerns the enactment of Yahweh's sovereignty. The dominant theme of this literature is deliverance by Yahweh, for which Israel is profoundly grateful. Israel was able to see that it was by David's hand that deliverance was wrought in Israel. Israel also knows, however, that beyond David, the real agent of deliverance is always and everywhere the God of Israel (cf. 1 Sam. 17:34–37)."—Brueggemann, *First and Second Samuel*, Interpretation, 339.

This is, as Brueggemann says, "covenant language" (Brueggemann, 340–41). Covenant relationship overcomes the chaos that threatens to send life back into the deep darkness from which the Creator formed it, to make of it the nonsense conveyed by the Hebrew *tohu wabohu* of Genesis 1:2 (rendered by NRSV as "formless void"). "Israel cried out . . . God heard their voice" creates a pattern that runs indomitably throughout the story of the people of God. It becomes in the telling a kind of creed, declaring faith's reliance on God to deliver, rescue, and set free people entrapped by their own behavior or oppressed by the greed and desires of others.

A cry for help and God, infinitely more faithful than we, keeps faith with our covenant. Verses 8–20 make clear to what lengths God goes to save God's people. In graphic, cosmic language the poet depicts YHWH literally moving heaven and earth to reach the embattled David. Lightning, fire, thunder, earthquake, and darkness—all the elements of creation are engaged to make way for Sovereign YHWH to leave the heavenly throne and come down in response to David's plea. It is a magnificent scene, artistically drawn to convey a profound truth about the Holy One who so graciously calls us into relationship. Imagine! The Creator of heaven and earth, loving humankind so passionately that our cries of chaos and distress, of fear and pain, for freedom and salvation move this Covenanting Sovereign to come to us and stand with us, defending and delivering us, restoring us to hope. This was David's faith; this is ours.

We know there is even more to this wonderful song. We have a story to tell of God coming to us, too. This time God's approaching is not told by earthquake, wind, and fire, but just as surely the "foundations of the earth were laid bare" (v. 16). Instead, God's coming is announced by a choir of angels to a group of startled shepherds keeping watch over their flocks at night (Luke 2). God comes this time as a baby, born in a feeding trough in "the city of David." This child, we proclaim, is the Christ, the Messiah, born to set all people free, to rescue and deliver us all from oppression and death's terrible threat of nothingness. This child, Jesus of Nazareth, is God Incarnate, God With Us. God the Spirit still broods over a new creation being formed for love, justice, and peace among all in whom God delights. The cry overcoming death we know in our story is one from the cross of the crucified Savior, hammered by our injustice and exposed to the depths of our inhumanity. Like David, our story of chaotic living does not end ensnared to deadly Sheol and drowning in hopelessness. The cross gives way to the empty tomb, and the miracle of God's will for us to live shines resolute on Easter morning.

Are our enemies—within and without—mere aberrations then? Is the pain of humanity, the oppression of hunger, the fear of violence, and the chaos of family abuse and personal despair—is this all only make-believe, since we seem only a word away from rescue and salvation? Ask David. Ask Jesus. Our passage is clear enough on this score, particularly since the hymn, as David's song, is retrospective.

Covenant love does not take covenant relationship with God for granted. The threats to a good life as God intends it are very real for us; the psalm urges us with its dark tones to take them very seriously. Chaos is, after all, the unraveling of God's creation, and Sheol the place where God is not. The mythic language abounding in this poem aims not to tell less truth but more. It stretches beyond the limits of ordinary speech to join heaven and earth and God and God's people together in one poetic voice. Truth be told, there is no way to tell it fully. Mythic imagery helps; poetry gives voice. But it is by faith that we may sing as surely as David, "He reached down from on high, he took me, he drew me out of the mighty waters" (v. 17). New birth comes out of waters like these.

I have concentrated our attention in this unit on verses 2–20 because the themes of David's song and the verses we may sing are focused here. The verses beyond these twenty are not unimportant by any means, but they carry through in many ways earlier harmonies. This is particularly true of verses 29–51, which appear to pick up on the images of God's coming to David's aid in the cataclysmic effort of God's coming to earth. David, as throughout the narrative of Samuel, is God's instrument through whom victory for God's people over the enemies who would destroy them is carried out. The repeated "I" of the celebration of David's victories, which we have heard in narrative accounts long before here, is in every case, explicitly or implicitly, preceded by David's confession of faith

> ## 📖 Want to Know More?
>
> **About apocalyptic literature?** See M. Eugene Boring, *Revelation*, Interpretation (Louisville, Ky.: John Knox Press, 1989), 35–46; William Barclay, *At the Last Trumpet: Jesus Christ and the End of Time* (Louisville, Ky.: Westminster John Knox Press, 1998), 1–17, 85–93.
>
> **About music in worship?** Robert H. Mitchell, *Ministry and Music* (Philadelphia: Westminster Press, 1978).
>
> **About the concept of *sheol* in the Old Testament?** See Horst Dietrich Preuss, *Old Testament Theology*, vol. 1, Old Testament Library (Louisville, Ky.: Westminster John Knox Press, 1995), 261–63; Walther Eichrodt, *Theology of the Old Testament*, vol. 2, Old Testament Library (Philadelphia: Westminster Press, 1967), 210–16.

that such empowerment comes to him "by you" (v. 30). David knows he cannot be his own savior; he has no power to save himself or others apart from God's promise, training, and equipping. We know that such is the case for us, too. David's song is ours again.

These solid images of preparation for battle have wonderful possibility as metaphors to help us think through God's empowering of us to meet the forces that, again in Luther's words, "threaten to undo us." The writer of Ephesians, himself spilling over into cosmic language to try to capture the threats and enemies he saw surrounding early Christians, admonishes readers, "Take up the whole armor of God, so that you may be able to withstand on that evil day, and having done everything, to stand firm" (Eph. 6:13). The undoing of faith that the writer worries about is a worry appropriate for us, too. The threat comes from what could be called "disciple amnesia." This is forgetting just what David remembers: that faith affirms that God saves; that we do not save ourselves; that God's gift of faith is a gift of relationship with God and the children of God to which God is steadfastly faithful. The gift of faith, with its promise of constancy from God, nonetheless is a covenant calling for response. Steadfastness, constancy, loyalty, keeping God's word—all these participate in the righteousness of relationship with God. We know from Samuel's stories that David does not always stand so firm or act in righteousness. So the teaching of 2 Samuel 22:21–28, which our poet ironically forces David to recite, does not fit easily into David's mouth—not apart from God's grace and power to make it so, despite David's worst behavior. That too, finally, is our case.

As I've noted already, this Song of David joins with the Song of Hannah in 1 Samuel 2 to mark a hymnic celebration opening and closing the books of Samuel. With a final word for our study, let us reach forward to another hymn that, like chapter 22, connects itself with Hannah. This one is Mary's song, and a wonderful note on which to end:

> My soul magnifies the Lord,
>   And my spirit rejoices in God, my Savior,
> For he has looked with favor on the lowliness of his servant.
>   Surely, from now on all generations will call me blessed;
> for the Mighty One has done great things for me,
>   and holy is his name.
>
> (Luke 1:46b–49)

Amen. May it be so. Our lives depend on it.

? Questions for Reflection

1. Songs of praise such as this have contributed greatly to the hymns we sing in worship today. What words or phrases in this passage remind you of some of our more well-known hymns?

2. In this unit we are asked: "Are our enemies . . . mere aberrations then? Is the pain of humanity, the oppression of hunger, the fear of violence, and the chaos of family abuse and personal despair— is this all only make-believe, since we seem only a word away from rescue and salvation?" How would you begin to answer this question?

3. It was stated that we can replace David's name with our name in verse 1, since David's song is our song, too. Do you feel that this song is your song? Why or why not?

4. In a sentence or two, talk about what you have learned over these past ten units about God's love for God's people.

Bibliography

Brueggemann, Walter. *First and Second Samuel.* Interpretation: A Bible Commentary for Teaching and Preaching. Louisville, Ky.: John Knox Press, 1990.

Carter, Stephen L. *Integrity.* New York: Basic Books, 1996.

Faulkner, William. *Absalom, Absalom!* 1936; New York: Random House, Modern Library, 1993.

Hertzberg, Hans Wilhelm. *I & II Samuel: A Commentary.* Louisville, Ky.: Westminster Press, 1964.

Hoge, Dean R., Benton Johnson, and Donald A. Luidens. *Vanishing Boundaries: The Religion of Mainline Baby Boomers.* Louisville, Ky.: Westminster John Knox Press, 1994.

McCarter, P. Kyle. *II Samuel: A New Translation with Introduction, Notes and Commentary.* Anchor Bible, vol. 9. New York: Doubleday & Co., 1984.

Newsom, Carol A., and Sharon H. Ringe, eds. *Women's Bible Commentary,* expanded edition. Louisville, Ky.: Westminster John Knox Press, 1998.

Newsome, James D., Jr. *1 & 2 Samuel,* Knox Preaching Guides. Atlanta: John Knox Press, 1982.

The Presbyterian Hymnal. Louisville, Ky.: Westminster John Knox Press, 1990.

Trible, Phyllis. *Texts of Terror: Literary-Feminist Readings of Biblical Narratives.* Philadelphia: Fortress Press, 1984.

Interpretation Bible Studies
Leader's Guide

Interpretation Bible Studies (IBS), for adults and older youth, are flexible, attractive, easy-to-use, and filled with solid information about the Bible. IBS helps Christians discover the guidance and power of the scriptures for living today. Perhaps you are leading a church school class, a mid-week Bible study group, or a youth group meeting, or simply using this in your own personal study. Whatever the setting may be, we hope you find this *Leader's Guide* helpful. Since every context and group is different, this *Leader's Guide* does not presume to tell you how to structure Bible study for your situation. Instead, the *Leader's Guide* seeks to offer choices—a number of helpful suggestions for leading a successful Bible study using IBS.

> "The church that no longer hears the essential message of the Scriptures soon ceases to understand what it is for and is open to be captured by the dominant religious philosophy of the moment."—James D. Smart, *The Strange Silence of the Bible in the Church: A Study in Hermeneutics* (Philadelphia: Westminster Press, 1970), 10.

How Should I Teach IBS?

1. Explore the Format

There is a wealth of information in IBS, perhaps more than you can use in one session. In this case, more is better. IBS has been designed to give you a well-stocked buffet of content and teachable insights. Pick and choose what suits your group's needs. Perhaps you will want to split units into two or more sessions, or combine units into a single session. Perhaps you will decide to use only a portion of a unit and then move on to the next unit. *There is not a structured theme or teaching focus to each unit that must be followed for IBS to be used.* Rather, IBS offers the flexibility to adjust to whatever suits your context.

"The more we bring to the Bible, the more we get from the Bible." —William Barclay, *A Beginner's Guide to the New Testament* (Louisville, Ky.: Westminster John Knox Press, 1995), vii.

Second, those who wish more specific suggestions for planning the sessions can find them at the Westminster John Knox Press Web site (**www.wjkbooks.com**). Here, you can access a study guide with teaching suggestions for each IBS unit as well as helpful quotations, selections from Bible dictionaries and encyclopedias, and other teaching helps.

IBS is not only teacher-friendly, it is also discussion-friendly. Given the opportunity, most adults and young people relish the chance to talk about the kind of issues raised in IBS. The secret, then, is to determine what works with your group, what will get them to talk. Several good methods for stimulating discussion are presented in this *Leader's Guide,* and once you learn your group, you can apply one of these methods and get the group discussing the Bible and its relevance in their lives.

The format of every IBS unit consists of several features:

a. Body of the Unit. This is the main content, consisting of interesting and informative commentary on the passage and scholarly insight into the biblical text and its significance for Christians today.

b. Sidebars. These are boxes that appear scattered throughout the body of the unit, with maps, photos, quotations, and intriguing ideas. Some sidebars can be identified quickly by a symbol, or icon, that helps the reader know what type of information can be found in that sidebar. There are icons for illustrations, key terms, pertinent quotes, and more.

c. Want to Know More? Each unit includes a "Want to Know More?" section that guides learners who wish to dig deeper and consult other resources. If your church library does not have the resources mentioned, you can look up the information in other standard Bible dictionaries, encyclopedias, and handbooks, or you can find much of this information at the Geneva Press Web site (see last page of this Guide).

d. Questions for Reflection. The unit ends with questions to help the learners think more deeply about the biblical passage and its pertinence for today. These questions are provided as examples only, and teachers are encouraged both to develop their own list of questions and to gather questions from the group. These discussion questions do not usually have specific "correct" answers. Again, the flexibility of IBS allows you to use these questions at the end of the group time, at the beginning, interspersed throughout, or not at all.

2. Select a Teaching Method

Here are ten suggestions. The format of IBS allows you to choose what direction you will take as you plan to teach. Only you will know how your lesson should best be designed for your group. Some adult groups prefer the lecture method, while others prefer a high level of free-ranging discussion. Many youth groups like interaction, activity, the use of music, and the chance to talk about their own experiences and feelings. Here is a list of a few possible approaches. Let your own creativity add to the list!

> "The trick is to make the Bible our book." — Duncan S. Ferguson, *Bible Basics: Mastering the Content of the Bible* (Louisville, Ky.: Westminster John Knox Press, 1995), 3.

a. Let's Talk about What We've Learned. In this approach, all group members are requested to read the scripture passage and the IBS unit before the group meets. Ask the group members to make notes about the main issues, concerns, and questions they see in the passage. When the group meets, these notes are collected, shared, and discussed. This method depends, of course, on the group's willingness to do some "homework."

b. What Do We Want and Need to Know? This approach begins by having the whole group read the scripture passage together. Then, drawing from your study of the IBS, you, as the teacher, write on a board or flip chart two lists:

(1) Things we should know to better understand this passage (content information related to the passage, for example, historical insights about political contexts, geographical landmarks, economic nuances, etc.), and

(2) Four or five "important issues we should talk about regarding this passage" (with implications for today—how the issues in the biblical context continue into today, for example, issues of idolatry or fear).

Allow the group to add to either list, if they wish, and use the lists to lead into a time of learning, reflection, and discussion. This approach is suitable for those settings where there is little or no advanced preparation by the students.

> "Although small groups can meet for many purposes and draw upon many different resources, the one resource which has shaped the life of the Church more than any other throughout its long history has been the Bible." —Roberta Hestenes, *Using the Bible in Groups* (Philadelphia: Westminster Press, 1983), 14.

c. Hunting and Gathering. Start the unit by having the group read the scripture passage together. Then divide the group into smaller clusters (perhaps having as few as one person), each with a different assignment. Some clusters can discuss one or more of the "Questions for Reflection." Others can look up key terms or people in a Bible dictionary or track down other biblical references found in the body of the unit. After the small clusters have had time to complete their tasks, gather the entire group again and lead them through the study mate-rial, allowing each cluster to contribute what it learned.

d. From Question Mark to Exclamation Point. This approach begins with contemporary questions and then moves to the biblical content as a response to those questions. One way to do this is for you to ask the group, at the beginning of the class, a rephrased version of one or more of the "Questions for Reflection" at the end of the study unit. For example, one of the questions at the end of the unit on Exodus 3:1–4:17 in the IBS *Exodus* volume reads,

> Moses raised four protests, or objections, to God's call. Contemporary people also raise objections to God's call. In what ways are these similar to Moses' protests? In what ways are they different?

This question assumes familiarity with the biblical passage about Moses, so the question would not work well before the group has explored the passage. However, try rephrasing this question as an opening exercise; for example:

> Here is a thought experiment: Let's assume that God, who called people in the Bible to do daring and risky things, still calls people today to tasks of faith and courage. In the Bible, God called Moses from a burning bush and called Isaiah in a moment of ecstatic worship in the Temple. How do you think God's call is experienced by people today? Where do you see evidence of people saying "yes" to God's call? When

people say "no" or raise an objection to God's call, what reasons do they give (to themselves, to God)?

Posing this or a similar question at the beginning will generate discussion and raise important issues, and then it can lead the group into an exploration of the biblical passage as a resource for thinking even more deeply about these questions.

e. Let's Go to the Library. From your church library, your pastor's library, or other sources, gather several good commentaries on the book of the Bible you are studying. Among the trustworthy commentaries are those in the Interpretation series (John Knox Press) and the Westminster Bible Companion series (Westminster John Knox Press). Divide your group into smaller clusters and give one commentary to each cluster (one or more of the clusters can be given the IBS volume instead of a full-length commentary). Ask each cluster to read the biblical passage you are studying and then to read the section of the commentary that covers that passage (if your group is large, you may want to make photocopies of the commentary material with proper permission, of course). The task of each cluster is to name the two or three most important insights they discover about the biblical passage by reading and talking together about the commentary material. When you reassemble the larger group to share these insights, your group will gain not only a variety of insights about the passage but also a sense that differing views of the same text are par for the course in biblical interpretation.

f. Working Creatively Together. Begin with a creative group task, tied to the main thrust of the study. For example, if the study is on the Ten Commandments, a parable, or a psalm, have the group rewrite the Ten Commandments, the parable, or the psalm in contemporary language. If the passage is an epistle, have the group write a letter to their own congregation. Or if the study is a narrative, have the group role-play the characters in the story or write a page describing the story from the point of view of one of the characters. After completion of the task, read and discuss the biblical passage, asking for interpretations and applications from the group and tying in IBS material as it fits the flow of the discussion.

g. Singing Our Faith. Begin the session by singing (or reading) together a hymn that alludes to the biblical passage being studied (or to the theological themes in the passage). For example, if you are studying the unit from the IBS volume on Psalm 121, you can sing "I to the Hills Will Lift My Eyes," "Sing Praise to God, Who Reigns Above," or another hymn based on Psalm 121. Let the group reflect on the thoughts and feelings evoked by the hymn, then move to the biblical passage, allowing the biblical text and the IBS material to underscore, clarify, refine, and deepen the discussion stimulated by the hymn. If you are ambitious, you may ask the group to write a new hymn at the end of the study! (Many hymnals have indexes in the back or companion volumes that help the user match hymns to scripture passages or topics.)

h. Fill in the Blanks. In order to help the learners focus on the content of the biblical passage, at the beginning of the session ask each member of the group to read the biblical passage and fill out a brief questionnaire about the details of the passage (provide a copy for each learner or write the questions on the board). For example, if you are studying the unit in the IBS *Matthew* volume on Matthew 22:1–14, the questionnaire could include questions such as the following:

—In this story, Jesus compares the kingdom of heaven to what?
—List the various responses of those who were invited to the king's banquet but who did not come.
—When his invitation was rejected, how did the king feel? What did the king do?
—In the second part of the story, when the king saw a man at the banquet without a wedding garment, what did the king say? What did the man say? What did the king do?
—What is the saying found at the end of this story?

Gather the group's responses to the questions and perhaps encourage discussion. Then lead the group through the IBS material helping the learners to understand the meanings of these details and the significance of the passage for today. Feeling creative? Instead of a fill-in-the-blanks questionnaire, create a crossword puzzle from names and words in the biblical passage.

i. Get the Picture. In this approach, stimulate group discussion by incorporating a painting, photograph, or other visual object into the lesson. You can begin by having the group examine and comment on this visual or you can introduce the visual later in the lesson—it depends on the object used. If, for example, you are studying the unit Exodus 3:1–4:17 in the IBS *Exodus* volume, you may want to view Paul Koli's very colorful painting *The Burning Bush*. Two sources for this painting are *The Bible Through Asian Eyes*, edited by Masao Takenaka and Ron O'Grady (National City, Calif.: Pace Publishing Co., 1991), and *Imaging the Word: An Arts and Lectionary Resource*, vol. 3, edited by Susan A. Blain (Cleveland: United Church Press, 1996).

j. Now Hear This. Especially if your class is large, you may want to use the lecture method. As the teacher, you prepare a presentation on the biblical passage, using as many resources as you have available plus your own experience, but following the content of the IBS unit as a guide. You can make the lecture even more lively by asking the learners at various points along the way to refer to the visuals and quotes found in the "sidebars." A place can be made for questions (like the ones at the end of the unit)—either at the close of the lecture or at strategic points along the way.

> "It is . . . important to call a Bible study group back to what the text being discussed actually says, especially when an individual has gotten off on some tangent." — Richard Robert Osmer, *Teaching for Faith: A Guide for Teachers of Adult Classes* (Louisville, Ky.: Westminster John Knox Press, 1992), 71.

3. Keep These Teaching Tips in Mind

There are no surefire guarantees for a teaching success. However, the following suggestions can increase the chances for a successful study:

a. Always Know Where the Group Is Headed. Take ample time beforehand to prepare the material. Know the main points of the study, and know the destination. Be flexible, and encourage discussion, but don't lose sight of where you are headed.

b. Ask Good Questions; Don't Be Afraid of Silence. Ideally, a discussion blossoms spontaneously from the reading of the scripture. But more often than not, a discussion must be drawn from the group members by a series of well-chosen questions. After asking each question, give the group members time to answer. Let them think, and don't be threatened by a season of silence. Don't feel that every question must have an answer, and that as leader, you must supply every answer. Facilitate discussion by getting the group members to cooperate with each other. Sometimes, the original question can be restated. Sometimes it is helpful to ask a follow-up question like "What makes this a hard question to answer?"

Ask questions that encourage explanatory answers. Try to avoid questions that can be answered simply "Yes" or "No." Rather than asking, "Do you think Moses was frightened by the burning bush?" ask, "What do you think Moses was feeling and experiencing as he stood before the burning bush?" If group members answer with just one word, ask a follow-up question like "Why do you think this is so?" Ask questions about their feelings and opinions, mixed within questions about facts or details. Repeat their responses or restate their response to reinforce their contributions to the group.

Most studies can generate discussion by asking open-ended questions. Depending on the group, several types of questions can work. Some groups will respond well to content questions that can be answered from reading the IBS comments or the biblical passage. Others will respond well to questions about feelings or thoughts. Still others will respond to questions that challenge them to new thoughts or that may not have exact answers. Be sensitive to the group's dynamic in choosing questions.

> "Studies of learning reveal that while people remember approximately 10% of what they hear, they remember up to 90% of what they say. Therefore, to increase the amount of learning that occurs, increase the amount of talking about the Bible which each member does." —Roberta Hestenes, *Using the Bible in Groups* (Philadelphia: Westminster Press, 1983), 17.

Some suggested questions are: What is the point of the passage? Who are the main characters? Where is the tension in the story? Why does it say (this)_____, and not (that) _____? What raises questions for you? What terms need defining? What are the new ideas? What doesn't make sense? What bothers or troubles you about this passage? What keeps you from living the truth of this passage?

c. Don't Settle for the Ordinary. There is nothing like a surprise. Think of special or unique ways to present the ideas of the study. Upset the applecart of the ordinary. Even though the passage may be familiar, look for ways to introduce suspense. Remember that a little mystery can capture the imagination. Change your routine.

Along with the element of surprise, humor can open up a discussion. Don't be afraid to laugh. A well-chosen joke or cartoon may present the central theme in a way that a lecture would have stymied.

Sometimes a passage is too familiar. No one speaks up because everyone feels that all that could be said has been said. Choose an unfamiliar translation from which to read, or if the passage is from a Gospel, compare the story across two or more Gospels and note differences. It is amazing what insights can be drawn from seeing something strange in what was thought to be familiar.

d. Feel Free to Supplement the IBS Resources with Other Material. Consult other commentaries or resources. Tie in current events with the lesson. Scour newspapers or magazines for stories that touch on the issues of the study. Sometimes the lyrics of a song, or a section of prose from a well-written novel will be just the right seasoning for the study.

e. And Don't Forget to Check the Web. You can download a free study guide from our Web site (**www.wjkbooks.com**). Each study guide includes several possibilities for applying the teaching methods suggested above for individual IBS units.

f. Stay Close to the Biblical Text. Don't forget that the goal is to learn the Bible. Return to the text again and again. Avoid making the mistake of reading the passage only at the beginning of the study, and then wandering away to comments on top of comments from that point on. Trust in the power and presence of the Holy Spirit to use the truths of the passage to work within the lives of the study participants.

> "The Bible is literature, but it is much more than literature. It is the holy book of Jews and Christians, who find there a manifestation of God's presence." —Kathleen Norris, *The Psalms* (New York: Riverhead Books, 1997), xxii.

What If I Am Using IBS in Personal Bible Study?

If you are using IBS in your personal Bible study, you can experiment and explore a variety of ways. You may choose to read straight through the study without giving any attention to the sidebars or other features. Or you may find yourself interested in a question or unfamiliar with a key term, and you can allow the sidebars "Want to Know More?" and "Questions for Reflection" to lead you into deeper learning on these issues. Perhaps you will want to have a few commentaries or a Bible dictionary available to pursue what interests you.

As was suggested in one of the teaching methods above, you may want to begin with the questions at the end, and then read the Bible passage followed by the IBS material. Trust the IBS resources to provide good and helpful information, and then follow your interests!

Want to Know More?

About leading Bible study groups? See Roberta Hestenes, *Using the Bible in Groups* (Philadelphia: Westminster Press, 1983).

About basic Bible content? See Duncan S. Ferguson, *Bible Basics: Mastering the Content of the Bible* (Louisville, Ky.: Westminster John Knox Press, 1995); William M. Ramsay, *The Westminster Guide to the Books of the Bible* (Louisville, Ky.: Westminster John Knox Press, 1994).

About the development of the Bible? See John Barton, *How the Bible Came to Be* (Louisville, Ky.: Westminster John Knox Press, 1997).

About the meaning of difficult terms? See Donald K. McKim, *Westminster Dictionary of Theological Terms* (Louisville, Ky.: Westminster John Knox Press, 1996); Paul J. Achtemeier, *Harper's Bible Dictionary* (San Francisco: Harper & Row, 1985).

To download a free IBS study guide,

visit our Web site at

www.wjkbooks.com